COMPLETE POEMS OF EDGAR ALLAN

POE

THE AMERICAN POETS
EDITED BY LOUIS UNTERMEYER FOR
THE HERITAGE PRESS

COMPLETE POEMS OF EDGAR ALLAN
POE

PREPARED, AND EDITED WITH A COMMENTARY,

BY *LOUIS UNTERMEYER*; ILLUSTRATED WITH

LITHOGRAPHS BY *HUGO STEINER-PRAG*

THE HERITAGE PRESS, NEW YORK

The Editor's Introduction

THE GENTEEL LITERATI of the nineteenth century were not only
startled but affronted by two American poets whose genius chal-
lenged them with a bright if baleful originality. Yet, although
the two rebellious poets, Edgar Allan Poe and Walt Whitman,
were contemporary, simultaneously engaged in hack-work in
New York City, they had nothing but poverty and adverse criticism in common. It is doubtful that they would have cared for
each other; the bizarre individualism of Poe was the complete
antithesis of Whitman's rowdy camaraderie. Since the first edition of *Leaves of Grass* was not published until 1855, six years
after Poe's death, it is unlikely that Poe ever read anything of
Whitman's except, perhaps, some early unsigned journalistic
prose. But Whitman did not fail to record his estimate of Poe, an
appraisal which echoed that of the critics who had assailed the
immorality of both writers. "Almost without the first sign of
moral principle or of the simpler affections of the heart," wrote
Whitman, "Poe's verses illustrate an intense faculty for technical
and abstract beauty, with the rhyming art to excess, an incorri-
gible propensity toward nocturnal themes, a demoniac undertone
behind every page ... brilliant and dazzling, but with no heat ...
I wanted, and still want for poetry, the clear sun and the fresh air
blowing—the strength and power of health, not of delirium—
with always the background of the eternal moralities."

II

Poe's lack of "the eternal moralities" may be traced from the last
phases of his flight from reality through unstable youth to a
child's earliest sense of insecurity.

The son of two itinerant actors, Poe was born in Boston, Massachusetts, January 19, 1809. His father, who played minor roles
in a traveling stock company, disappeared shortly after his
second son was born—the first-born, William Henry Leonard,
was two years Edgar's senior. His mother, a frail dancer rather
than an accomplished actress, gave birth to a daughter Rosalie in
1810, and supported all three children in spite of increasing poverty and illness. A year after the birth of her third child the strain

was too much for her; she succumbed to pneumonia in Richmond, Virginia. The children were separated; William Henry Leonard had already been left in the care of his paternal grandfather; Rosalie was adopted by Mr. and Mrs. William Mackenzie; and Edgar was taken into the home of the Richmond merchant John Allan and his childless wife. Although the boy was only three years old the shock of death and the feeling of separateness must have shaken him profoundly. As Hervey Allen wrote in the monumental *Israfel: The Life and Times of Edgar Allan Poe*, "Even a child of three may be conscious at the time that his own little familiar world has gone to pieces about it. . . . He must have experienced for the first time the extreme sense of fear and utter loneliness which was to follow him to the grave." The sense of fear and growing insecurity was grave enough to the child; it increased with the knowledge that he was dependent upon a foster father who supported but never legally adopted him. As a result, the boy turned desperately to the childless Mrs. Allan, just as later in life the man turned to other women for love —not so much for love itself, but for love as protection against a world that seemed not only melancholy but malign.

III

In spite of the indictment of a few partisan biographers, John Allan was not a cruel foster-father. He loved children—the record shows he cared for at least two illegitimate sons—and he was particularly indulgent to young Edgar. When Poe was seven, Allan took him to England and placed him in one of the best schools—Poe pictured the place in the semi-autobiographical story "William Wilson." It was in England that he began to write; a poem, written at the age of twelve, reveals how early Poe was beginning to feel, and use, the abiding sense of loneliness and terror. The unhappy tone of "The Lake" does not differ greatly from the normal morbidity of adolescence, but the air is already heavy with Poe's peculiar and languorous music:

> But when Night had thrown her pall
> Upon that spot, as upon all,
> And the mystic wind went by
> Murmuring in melody—

Then—ah, then, I would awake
To the terror of the lone lake.

Death was in that poisonous wave,
And in its gulf a fitting grave
For him who thence could solace bring
To his lone imagining . . .

Full of "lone imagining" Poe returned to America. At sixteen
he fell platonically but passionately in love with Mrs. Stanard,
mother of one of his friends. The dark-eyed, mother-seeking
youth and the highly sensitive woman who died of insanity a
few years later did not meet often, but often enough to inspire the
unforgettable lyric which begins: "Helen, thy beauty is to me."
Although Poe said he haunted Mrs. Stanard's grave for years, he
made love to the fifteen-year-old Sarah Elmira Royster, but their
letters were intercepted; Poe entered the University of Virginia
and, a few months later, Sarah Elmira was married to a Mr.
Shelton.

It was at the University of Virginia that Poe was trapped by
the combination of weakness and recklessness which was even-
tually to undo him. Not a heavy drinker, he drank for excitement, to give himself a confidence that was as temporary as it
was false. In a day when drinking was common, indeed almost a
part of the curriculum, Poe drank badly. He gambled, lost consistently, and was unable to pay his bills. When his foster-father
refused to meet his debts, Poe was obliged to leave the University.
Returning home, he quarreled with Allan, and ran away from
Richmond.

The legend still persists that Poe left the United States and
set out for Europe (according to one of his biographers, "with the
intention of assisting the Greeks, then struggling to free themselves from the intolerable yoke of Turkey"), that he fought a
duel in France, that he was arrested in the gutters of St. Peters-
burg, and was saved only by the intervention of the American
Consulate in Russia. Researchers in the War Department have
disposed of that mythical European adventure. It is now clear
that Poe made a hurried trip to Boston and spent what little
money he had on the publication of his first volume *Tamerlane*,

and Other Poems. He then falsified his age, stating he was twenty-two although he was only eighteen, changed his name to Edgar A. Perry, and enlisted in the United States Army. The record gives his height as five feet, eight inches; his complexion fair; his hair brown; and his eyes grey.

IV

Poe remained in the United States Army from 1827 to 1829, from his eighteenth to his twentieth year, rebellious most of the time. Fortunately, Allan was able to procure his discharge, and Poe returned to Richmond, where he patched up his differences with his foster-father. Within a few weeks Poe's "imp of the perverse" drove him to fresh quarrels and renewed protestations of regret. Finally, in another effort to "reform," Poe entered West Point in his twenty-second year. Six months later he was dismissed for disobeying orders and gross neglect of duty.

Poe was a month more than twenty-two when he came to New York to enter another phase of his long struggle against oblivion. He had seventy-five cents in his pocket and no prospects; he was nervously ill; the marks of "the weary, wayworn wanderer" were already upon him. For two years he did the lowest forms of hack-work and never had quite enough to eat. He thought of various escapes—of going to Paris and enlisting as a soldier of fortune, of staying at home and becoming a school-teacher—but he still hoped to make a career as a poet. When that hope faded and a revision of his *Poems* went unnoticed, Poe went to live with his aunt Mrs. Maria Poe Clemm in Baltimore. The motherly Mrs. Clemm was already taking care of a young daughter, Virginia, and Poe's brother, William Henry; but she welcomed the dependent outcast and, somehow, provided for him. A few months after Poe arrived in Baltimore, William Henry died of tuberculosis. Four years later, Poe married his cousin. He was twenty-seven years old; Virginia was thirteen.

V

At twenty-seven Poe was continually suffering from the effects of opium and nervous exhaustion. Days of wild exaltation were followed by weeks of depressive morbidity. Yet his creative energy was boundless. In one year he contributed eighty-three reviews, four essays, six poems, and three stories to the *Southern Literary Messenger*, of which he had become editor. But he could not hold a position; he was always being irregularly employed and regularly discharged. From Baltimore he went to Richmond, bringing Virginia with him, and Mrs. Clemm to look after them both. From Richmond they went to New York, then to Philadelphia, then back again to New York. There were brief periods of success though never of serenity. *The Narrative of Arthur Gordon Pym*, Poe's fourth volume, was published in New York and London; *Tales of the Grotesque and Arabesque* appeared in two volumes in Philadelphia; a prize of one hundred dollars was won with *The Gold Bug*, his most widely read story. This was in 1842, when Poe was thirty-three. From that time on he began to disintegrate. He disappeared for days and was brought home delirious; in debt to all his friends, he accused them of stealing his ideas; he saw plagiarism and persecution everywhere. "I became insane," he wrote some years later to a friend, "insane, with long intervals of horrible sanity. During these fits of absolute unconsciousness I drank—God only knows how often or how much. My enemies referred the insanity to the drink, rather than the drink to the insanity."

Meanwhile, the tireless Mrs. Clemm begged and borrowed, pleaded with editors for advance payments on stories which Poe had promised but had failed to deliver, received discreet contributions from the lady poets with whom Poe had indiscreetly flirted, and by sheer determination managed to keep the family together.

VI

In 1846 it was evident that Virginia, whom Poe always called "Sis," was desperately ill with consumption, and the Poes moved to a small workman's dwelling in Fordham, then "a little village thirteen miles out of town." The summer and autumn were bearable. But before winter had set in, the wolf howled across the sills of the bare cottage where Mrs. Clemm was patching rags and Virginia lay on a straw mattress in the attic, wrapped in Poe's old army coat. Poe could no longer afford stamps to mail his manuscripts, and Mrs. Clemm had to borrow a few cents to get a letter from the postoffice. There were no blankets in the house, the stove was frequently without wood, and the dying consumptive hugged a large tortoise-shell cat to keep warm. Various ladies, including Mrs. Frances Sargent Osgood, to whom Poe had written pretty acrostic poems, collected a few comforts and some money for necessities, but it was too late. On a bitter cold night in January, at the age of twenty-four, Virginia coughed to death.

VII

Poe was now thirty-eight. His nerves were constantly twitching; his heart was giving out; he kept himself alive with work and morphine. Although Mrs. Clemm still mothered him, he sought companionship, and possibly marriage, among the lady literati. Mrs. Osgood was married; and, though she had sentimentalized over Poe, she was unwilling to sacrifice herself or her reputation for him. Poe paid court to Mrs. Marie Louise Shew, who had helped Virginia to die in decency and had taken care of Poe during his subsequent collapse; but Mrs. Shew was too practical a person to unite herself with a febrile romanticist. Poe next turned to Sarah Helen Whitman, "the seeress of Providence"; the widow was well-to-do and seven years older than Poe. There was a passionate correspondence, a mixture of urgency and literary affectation, and Mrs. Whitman indicated that she would marry him. As soon as she consented, Poe found himself madly in love with Mrs. Annie Richmond, who inspired "For Annie" and "Annabel Lee." Unable to give up either woman, Poe attempted suicide by swallowing an ounce of laudanum and was saved only because the overdose acted as an emetic. Mrs. Whitman broke off the engagement, and once more Poe went to pieces.

Eureka, the tenth and last of Poe's books to appear during his lifetime, caused something of a sensation with its mingling of brilliant intuition, wild mysticism, and pseudo-scientific plausibility. But although Poe was famous, he was destitute. He roamed about aimlessly, sustained by the dream of a great national magazine and the hope of finding a domestic haven. In Richmond he met Sara Elmira Shelton, his boyhood sweetheart, now the widow of a successful merchant, and he immediately began to woo her. It was a strange courtship; but the placid church-going widow was fluttered when Poe recalled their childhood romance and told her she was his "lost Lenore." She promised to provide a home not only for him but for Mrs. Clemm, as well as funds for the magazine which Poe was to launch. Going north to bring Mrs. Clemm back to Richmond for the marriage, Poe stopped off at Baltimore. There he disappeared. Five days later he was discovered in a bar-room, surrounded by hoodlums, "his face haggard, not to say bloated, his hair unkempt, and his whole physique repulsive." He was taken to the Washington College Hospital and there he tossed, called to specters "that withered and loomed on the walls." He remained in delirium five days, and it was not until Sunday, October 7, 1849, that he recovered consciousness, cried out, "Lord help my soul," and died. He was in his forty-first year when the doctor pulled the sheet over his tortured face.

VIII

This is not the place to appraise Poe's importance as critic, prophet, essayist, short-story writer, father of modern detective fiction and tales of ratiocination. Poe was, first of all, a poet. "With me," he declared, "poetry has not been a purpose, but a passion," and some effort must be made to reconcile the contradictions of his poetic genius. James Russell Lowell's much-quoted couplet is not wholly a gibe:

> There comes Poe with his raven like Barnaby Rudge;
> Three fifths of him genius and two fifths sheer fudge.

The "sheer fudge" is all too aparent: the florid tone, the elaborate tastelessness, the Gothic theatrical claptrap, the gaudy proper names: the flashiness of Guy de Vere, Eulalie, Ulalume, D'Elormie (invented because it rhymed with "bore me") and Yaanek (to match "Titanic"), the overemphasized metres that din themselves into burlesque, and the "sense swooning into nonsense."

Against this there must be measured a poetry of pure incantation, a poetry whose power is hypnotic. Poe knew exactly what he was doing when he blurred the meaning of a stanza and substituted verbal excitement for rational content. His was a tensity of sensation heightened by pure suggestiveness; he conceived (as he said of Hawthorne) "with deliberate care a certain unique or single effect," and plunged the reader into a world of dreams— or, to be more exact, "a dream within a dream."

This wavering indefiniteness, this sense of unreality, was what Poe was always intent upon achieving. In the famous "Letter to B—" he announced his purpose in a paraphrase from Coleridge: "A poem, in my opinion, is opposed to a work of science by having, for its *immediate* object, pleasure, not truth; to romance by having, for its object, an *indefinite* instead of a definite pleasure, being a poem only so far as this object is attained." Poe's effort to charge every line with indefinite sensations ("to which end music is an essential, since the comprehension of sweet sound is our most indefinite conception") sometimes resulted in the expression of strong feeling, sometimes in a parody of emotion. Two lines from Ulalume are significant:

> It was night in the lonesome October
> Of my most immemorial year.

"Here," says Saintsbury, "it would puzzle the most adroit student of words to attach a distinct usual sense to 'immemorial.' And yet no one with an ear can fail to see that it is emphatically the right word and supplies the necessary note of suggestion."

That is Poe's chief contribution to American poetry: "the necessary note of suggestion." It is the note of unreasoning enchantment, of pure trance which echoes throughout Poe's verse—

> In what ethereal dances
> By what eternal streams!

It is true that Poe limited the scope of his poetry by binding it to a theory. The insistence that "a certain taint of sadness is inseparably connected with the higher manifestations of beauty" makes for a morbid monotone and "taints" the verse with funereal reveries. Poe was obsessed with death—with death and beauty ("the death of a beautiful woman is, unquestionably, the most poetical topic in the world"), with death and cheated desire, with death and cruelty, with death and the horror of dissolution.

xvi

The tales as well as the poems play variations on the theme; the music seems to rise from valleys of despair, dark tarns, ghoul-haunted palaces; even the light fantasies turn into black phantasmagoria.

But the magic persists, the magic of one who is, as Poe characterized his own "Politian,"

> ... a dreamer, and a man shut out
> From common passions.

Shut out from "common passions," Poe's lines have almost nothing to do with the concerns of every day. Whitman, that strong son of light, was not wrong; Poe's verses are "nocturnal," for Poe was one of the children of the night. Here he triumphs; in the limbo between consciousness and unreality Poe is supreme. His poetry has the vagueness of a dream: "out of space, out of time." It is illogical and inconclusive, but—like a dream—it is often more poignant, and sometimes more persuasive, than reality.

The Table of Contents

V

THE POETIC PRINCIPLE

VI

POEMS ADDED IN THE EDITION OF 1845

VII

THE RATIONALE OF VERSE

VIII

POEMS COLLECTED AFTER 1845

[THE TABLE OF CONTENTS]

IX

THE PHILOSOPHY OF COMPOSITION

A List of the Lithographs

The Poems of Edgar Allan Poe

I

POEMS WRITTEN BEFORE 1827

The Editor's Commentary

POE WAS EIGHTEEN IN 1827 when he published his first volume, *Tamerlane and Other Poems*. Between forty and fifty copies were issued by a job printer and it is doubtful that they were ever circulated. Only four copies are known to be in existence today.

The title page named no author, but merely stated that the book was "By a Bostonian." There are two possible reasons for the anonymity: Poe wanted to keep his whereabouts unknown, for he was running away from debts; he also hoped that a certain mysteriousness might pique the reviewers, especially if the book came from Boston—center of the New England coterie—where the anonymous poet might, perhaps, turn out to be another Longfellow. Some evidence that the runaway Poe had the first reason in mind is the motto from Cowper which Poe placed on the title page:

> Young heads are giddy, and young hearts are warm,
> And make mistakes for manhood to reform.

Lest this couplet might seem too apologetic, Poe followed it with a Preface which was less modest. Most of the poems, said Poe, were composed before the author had completed his fourteenth year, and although he was conscious that there may be faults, "which he flatters himself he could with little trouble have corrected, unlike many of his predecessors, he has been too fond of his early productions to amend them in his *old age*."

Nevertheless, Poe was quick to amend his verse; few poets have been more diligent in revision and none has succeeded so well. For example, in "A Dream within a Dream" two lines originally appeared:

> I am standing 'mid the roar
> Of a weather-beaten shore.

Two years later the lines were changed to:

> I was standing 'mid the roar
> Of a wind-beaten shore.

But Poe was not satisfied until he had rephrased the lines so that they read:

> I stand amid the roar
> Of a surf-tormented shore.

That was the final version. The poet had put his personal stamp upon it; "surf-tormented" is the very essence of Poe.

Stanzas

How often we forget all time, when lone
Admiring Nature's universal throne;
Her woods—her wilds—her mountains—the intense
Reply of HERS *to* OUR *intelligence!* [BYRON, *The Island.*]

I

In youth have I known one with whom the Earth
In secret communing held—as he with it,
In daylight, and in beauty from his birth:
Whose fervid, flickering torch of life was lit
From the sun and stars, whence he had drawn forth
A passionate light—such for his spirit was fit—
And yet that spirit knew not, in the hour
Of its own fervor what had o'er it power.

II

Perhaps it may be that my mind is wrought
To a fever by the moonbeam that hangs o'er,
But I will half believe that wild light fraught
With more of sovereignty than ancient lore
Hath ever told—or is it of a thought
The unembodied essence, and no more,
That with a quickening spell doth o'er us pass
As dew of the night-time o'er the summer grass?

III

Doth o'er us pass, when, as th' expanding eye
To the loved object—so the tear to the lid
Will start, which lately slept in apathy?
And yet it need not be—(that object) hid
From us in life—but common—which doth lie
Each hour before us—but *then* only, bid
With a strange sound, as of a harp-string broken,
To awake us—'Tis a symbol and a token

IV

Of what in other worlds shall be—and given
In beauty by our God, to those alone
Who otherwise would fall from life and Heaven
Drawn by their heart's passion, and that tone,
That high tone of the spirit which hath striven,
Tho' not with Faith—with godliness—whose throne
With desperate energy 't hath beaten down;
Wearing its own deep feeling as a crown.

3.

Evening Star   'Twas noontide of summer,
        And mid-time of night;
    And stars, in their orbits,
        Shone pale, thro' the light
    Of the brighter, cold moon,
        'Mid planets her slaves,
    Herself in the Heavens,
        Her beam on the waves.
            I gazed awhile
            On her cold smile;
    Too cold—too cold for me—
        There pass'd, as a shroud,
        A fleecy cloud,
    And I turn'd away to thee,
        Proud Evening Star,
        In thy glory afar,
    And dearer thy beam shall be;
        For joy to my heart
        Is the proud part
    Thou bearest in Heaven at night,
        And more I admire
        Thy distant fire,
    Than that colder, lowly light.

Song   I saw thee on thy bridal day—
        When a burning blush came o'er thee,
    Though happiness around thee lay,
        The world all love before thee:

    And in thine eye a kindling light
        (Whatever it might be)
    Was all on Earth my aching sight
        Of Loveliness could see.

    That blush, perhaps, was maiden shame—
        As such it well may pass—
    Though its glow hath raised a fiercer flame
        In the breast of him, alas!

    Who saw thee on that bridal day,
        When that deep blush *would* come o'er thee,
    Though happiness around thee lay;
        The world all love before thee.

4

Tamerlane

Kind solace in a dying hour!
  Such, father, is not (now) my theme—
I will not madly deem that power
    Of Earth may shrive me of the sin
    Unearthly pride hath revell'd in—
  I have no time to dote or dream:
You call it hope—that fire of fire!
It is but agony of desire:
If I *can* hope—Oh God! I can—
  Its fount is holier—more divine—
I would not call thee fool, old man,
  But such is not a gift of thine.

Know thou the secret of a spirit
  Bow'd from its wild pride into shame.
O yearning heart! I did inherit
  Thy withering portion with the fame,
The searing glory which hath shone
Amid the jewels of my throne,
Halo of Hell! and with a pain
Not Hell shall make me fear again—
O craving heart, for the lost flowers
And sunshine of my summer hours!
The undying voice of that dead time,
With its interminable chime,
Rings, in the spirit of a spell,
Upon thy emptiness—a knell.

I have not always been as now:
The fever'd diadem on my brow
  I claim'd and won usurpingly—
Hath not the same fierce heirdom given
  Rome to the Caesar—this to me?
    The heritage of a kingly mind,
And a proud spirit which hath striven
    Triumphantly with human kind.

On mountain soil I first drew life:
  The mists of the Taglay have shed
  Nightly their dews upon my head,
And, I believe, the wingèd strife
And tumult of the headlong air
Have nestled in my very hair.

So late from Heaven—that dew—it fell
  ('Mid dreams of an unholy night)
Upon me with the touch of Hell,
    While the red flashing of the light
From clouds that hung, like banners, o'er,
    Appeared to my half-closing eye
    The pageantry of monarchy,
And the deep trumpet-thunder's roar
    Came hurriedly upon me, telling
      Of human battle, where my voice,
My own voice, silly child!—was swelling
    (O! how my spirit would rejoice,
And leap within me at the cry)
The battle-cry of Victory!

The rain came down upon my head
    Unshelter'd—and the heavy wind
    Rendered me mad and deaf and blind.
It was but man, I thought, who shed
    Laurels upon me: and the rush—
The torrent of the chilly air
    Gurgled within my ear the crush
Of empires—with the captive's prayer—
The hum of suitors—and the tone
Of flattery 'round a sovereign's throne.

My passions, from that hapless hour,
    Usurp'd a tyranny which men
Have deem'd, since I have reach'd to power,
      My innate nature—be it so:
    But father, there liv'd one who, then,
Then—in my boyhood—when their fire
      Burn'd with a still intenser glow,
(For passion must, with youth, expire)
    E'en *then* who knew this iron heart
    In woman's weakness had a part.

I have no words—alas!—to tell
The loveliness of loving well!
Nor would I now attempt to trace
The more than beauty of a face
Whose lineaments, upon my mind,
Are—shadows on th' unstable wind:
Thus I remember having dwelt

Some page of early lore upon,
With loitering eye, till I have felt
The letters—with their meaning—melt
    To fantasies—with none.

O, she was worthy of all love!
    Love—as in infancy was mine—
'Twas such as angel minds above
    Might envy; her young heart the shrine
On which my every hope and thought
    Were incense—then a goodly gift,
        For they were childish and upright—
Pure—as her young example taught:
    Why did I leave it, and, adrift,
        Trust to the fire within, for light?

We grew in age—and love—together,
    Roaming the forest, and the wild;
My breast her shield in wintry weather—
    And when the friendly sunshine smil'd,
And she would mark the opening skies,
I saw no Heaven—but in her eyes.

Young Love's first lesson is—the heart:
    For 'mid that sunshine, and those smiles,
When, from our little cares apart,
    And laughing at her girlish wiles,
I'd throw me on her throbbing breast,
    And pour my spirit out in tears—
There was no need to speak the rest—
    No need to quiet any fears
Of her—who ask'd no reason why,
But turn'd on me her quiet eye!

Yet *more* than worthy of the love
My spirit struggled with, and strove,
When, on the mountain peak, alone,
Ambition lent it a new tone—
I had no being—but in thee:
    The world, and all it did contain
In the earth—the air—the sea—
    Its joy—its little lot of pain
That was new pleasure—the ideal,
    Dim vanities of dreams by night—

And dimmer nothings which were real—
   (Shadows—and a more shadowy light!)
Parted upon their misty wings,
   And, so, confusedly, became
   Thine image, and—a name—a name!
Two separate—yet most intimate things.

I was ambitious—have you known
   The passion, father? You have not:
A cottager, I mark'd a throne
Of half the world as all my own,
   And murmur'd at such lowly lot—
But, just like any other dream,
   Upon the vapour of the dew
My own had past, did not the beam
   Of beauty which did while it thro'
The minute—the hour—the day—oppress
My mind with double loveliness.

We walk'd together on the crown
Of a high mountain which look'd down
Afar from its proud natural towers
   Of rock and forest, on the hills—
The dwindled hills! begirt with bowers,
   And shouting with a thousand rills.

I spoke to her of power and pride,
   But mystically—in such guise
That she might deem it nought beside
   The moment's converse; in her eyes
I read, perhaps too carelessly—
   A mingled feeling with my own—
The flush on her bright cheek, to me
   Seem'd to become a queenly throne
Too well that I should let it be
   Light in the wilderness alone.

I wrapp'd myself in grandeur then,
   And donn'd a visionary crown—
     Yet it was not that Fantasy
     Had thrown her mantle over me—
But that, among the rabble—men,
   Lion ambition is chained down—

And crouches to a keeper's hand—
Not so in deserts where the grand—
The wild—the terrible conspire
With their own breath to fan his fire.

Look 'round thee now on Samarcand!
   Is not she queen of Earth? her pride
Above all cities? in her hand
   Their destinies? in all beside
Of glory which the world hath known
Stands she not nobly and alone?
Falling—her veriest stepping-stone
Shall form the pedestal of a throne—
And who her sovereign? Timour—he
   Whom the astonished people saw
Striding o'er empires haughtily
   A diadem'd outlaw!

O, human love! thou spirit given
On Earth, of all we hope in Heaven!
Which fall'st into the soul like rain
Upon the Siroc-wither'd plain,
And, failing in thy power to bless,
But leav'st the heart a wilderness!
Idea! which bindest life around
With music of so strange a sound,
And beauty of so wild a birth—
Farewell! for I have won the Earth.

When Hope, the eagle that tower'd, could see
   No cliff beyond him in the sky,
His pinions were bent droopingly—
   And homeward turn'd his soften'd eye.
'Twas sunset: when the sun will part
There comes a sullenness of heart
To him who still would look upon
The glory of the summer sun.
That soul will hate the ev'ning mist,
So often lovely, and will list
To the sound of the coming darkness (known
To those whose spirits hearken) as one
Who, in a dream of night, *would* fly
But *cannot* from a danger nigh.

What tho' the moon—the white moon
Shed all the splendour of her noon,
Her smile is chilly, and *her* beam,
In that time of dreariness, will seem
(So like you gather in your breath)
A portrait taken after death.
And boyhood is a summer sun
Whose waning is the dreariest one—
For all we live to know is known,
And all we seek to keep hath flown—
Let life, then, as the day-flower, fall
With the noon-day beauty—which is all.

I reach'd my home—my home no more
    For all had flown who made it so.
I pass'd from out its mossy door,
    And, tho' my tread was soft and low,
A voice came from the threshold stone
Of one whom I had earlier known—
    O, I defy thee, Hell, to show
    On beds of fire that burn below,
    A humbler heart—a deeper woe.

Father, I firmly do believe—
    I *know*—for Death, who comes for me
        From regions of the blest afar,
Where there is nothing to deceive,
        Hath left his iron gate ajar,
    And rays of truth you cannot see
        Are flashing thro' Eternity——
I do believe that Eblis hath
A snare in every human path—
Else how, when in the holy grove
I wandered of the idol, Love,
Who daily scents his snowy wings
With incense of burnt offerings
From the most unpolluted things,
Whose pleasant bowers are yet so riven
Above with trellis'd rays from Heaven,
No mote may shun—no tiniest fly—
The lightning of his eagle eye—
How was it that Ambition crept,
    Unseen, amid the revels there,
Till growing bold, he laughed and leapt
    In the tangles of Love's very hair?

TAMERLANE

Dreams

Oh! that my young life were a lasting dream!
My spirit not awakening, till the beam
Of an Eternity should bring the morrow.
Yes! tho' that long dream were of hopeless sorrow,
'Twere better than the cold reality
Of waking life, to him whose heart must be,
And hath been still, upon the lovely earth,
A chaos of deep passion, from his birth.
But should it be—that dream eternally
Continuing—as dreams have been to me
In my young boyhood—should it thus be given,
'Twere folly still to hope for higher Heaven.
For I have revell'd, when the sun was bright
I' the summer sky, in dreams of living light
And loveliness,—have left my very heart
In climes of my imagining, apart
From mine own home, with beings that have been
Of mine own thought—what more could I have seen?
'Twas once—and only once—and the wild hour
From my remembrance shall not pass—some power
Or spell had bound me—'twas the chilly wind
Came o'er me in the night, and left behind
Its image on my spirit—or the moon
Shone on my slumbers in her lofty noon
Too coldly—or the stars—howe'er it was
That dream was as that night-wind—let it pass.

I *have been* happy, tho' in a dream.
I have been happy—and I love the theme:
Dreams! in their vivid coloring of life,
As in that fleeting, shadowy, misty strife
Of semblance with reality, which brings
To the delirious eye, more lovely things
Of Paradise and Love—and all our own!
Than young Hope in his sunniest hour hath known.

Spirits of the Dead

Thy soul shall find itself alone
'Mid dark thoughts of the grey tomb-stone;
Not one, of all the crowd, to pry
Into thine hour of secrecy.

Be silent in that solitude,
    Which is not loneliness—for then
The spirits of the dead, who stood
    In life before thee, are again
In death around thee, and their will
Shall overshadow thee; be still.

The night, though clear, shall frown,
And the stars shall not look down
From their high thrones in the Heaven
With light like hope to mortals given,
But their red orbs, without beam,
To thy weariness shall seem
As a burning and a fever
Which would cling to thee for ever.

Now are thoughts thou shalt not banish,
Now are visions ne'er to vanish;
From thy spirit shall they pass
No more, like dew-drop from the grass.

The breeze, the breath of God, is still,
And the mist upon the hill
Shadowy, shadowy, yet unbroken,
Is a symbol and a token.
How it hangs upon the trees,
A mystery of mysteries!

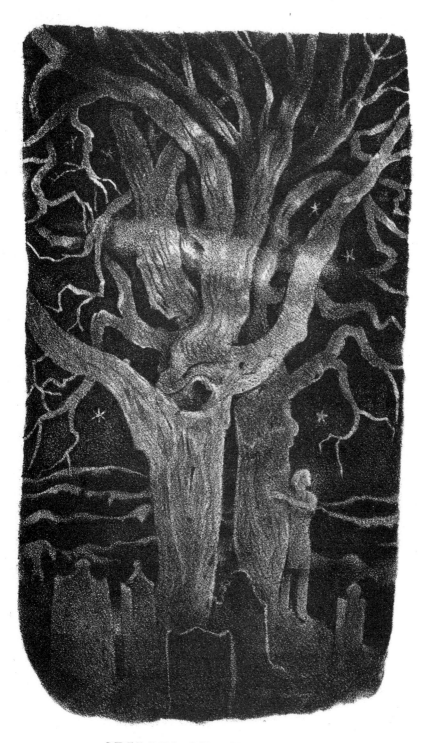

SPIRITS OF THE DEAD

A Dream within a Dream

Take this kiss upon the brow!
And, in parting from you now,
Thus much let me avow—
You are not wrong, who deem
That my days have been a dream;
Yet if hope has flown away
In a night, or in a day,
In a vision, or in none,
Is it therefore the less *gone*?
All that we see or seem
Is but a dream within a dream.

I stand amid the roar
Of a surf-tormented shore,
And I hold within my hand
Grains of the golden sand—
How few! yet how they creep
Through my fingers to the deep,
While I weep—while I weep!
O God! can I not grasp
Them with a tighter clasp?
O God! can I not save
One from the pitiless wave?
Is *all* that we see or seem
But a dream within a dream?

The Lake. To ———

In spring of youth it was my lot
To haunt of the wide world a spot
The which I could not love the less—
So lovely was the loneliness
Of a wild lake, with black rock bound,
And the tall pines that towered around.

But when the Night had thrown her pall
Upon that spot, as upon all,
And the mystic wind went by
Murmuring in melody—
Then—ah then I would awake
To the terror of the lone lake.

Yet that terror was not fright,
But a tremulous delight—
A feeling not the jewelled mine
Could teach or bribe me to define—
Nor Love—although the Love were thine.

Death was in that poisonous wave,
And in its gulf a fitting grave
For him who thence could solace bring
To his lone imagining—
Whose solitary soul could make
An Eden of that dim lake.

THE LAKE

The Happiest Day, the Happiest Hour

The happiest day—the happiest hour
　My sear'd and blighted heart hath known,
The highest hope of pride and power,
　I feel hath flown.

Of power! said I? yes! such I ween;
　But they have vanish'd long, alas!
The visions of my youth have been—
　But let them pass.

And, pride, what have I now with thee?
　Another brow may even inherit
The venom thou hast pour'd on me—
　Be still, my spirit!

The happiest day—the happiest hour
　Mine eyes shall see—have ever seen,
The brightest glance of pride and power,
　I feel—have been:

But were that hope of pride and power
　Now offer'd with the pain
Even *then* I felt—that brightest hour
　I would not live again:

For on its wing was dark alloy,
　And, as it flutter'd—fell
An essence—powerful to destroy
　A soul that knew it well.

A Dream

In visions of the dark night
    I have dreamed of joy departed—
But a waking dream of life and light
    Hath left me broken-hearted.

Ah! what is not a dream by day
    To him whose eyes are cast
On things around him with a ray
    Turned back upon the past?

That holy dream—that holy dream,
    While all the world were chiding,
Hath cheered me as a lovely beam
    A lonely spirit guiding.

What though that light, thro' storm and night,
    So trembled from afar—
What could there be more purely bright
    In Truth's day-star?

The Poems of Edgar Allan Poe

II

POEMS ADDED IN THE EDITION OF 1829

POE's SECOND VOLUME, *Al Aaraaf, Tamerlane, and Minor Poems,* was published in 1829, when the author was within a month of his twenty-first birthday. Most of the poems in the volume had appeared in his first book, but they had been considerably altered in the ensuing two and a half years. "Tamerlane" had been almost completely written and, half-concealed in its parable of Love against Power, it is not hard to detect Poe's unhappy wooing of Sarah Elmira Royster, who had become the well-to-do Mrs. Shelton.

The seven new poems are a mixture of pastiche and pure poetry. "Al Aaraaf" is a puzzle. It seems to be an allegory in which Beauty is ranked above Love, a cryptic poem to which the young poet appended erudite notes with obvious relish. One of Poe's editors suspects that in "Al Aaraaf" Poe may be perpetrating "a huge hoax, challenging the wits to vain attempts at solving that which has no solution." Yet "Al Aaraaf" contains many sonorous lines as well as the exquisite lyric to Ligeia; Poe was particularly fond of the imagery and sound of:

> There Nature speaks and even ideal things
> Flap shadowy sounds from visionary wings.

None of the poems added in the 1829 edition is as significant as "Romance." As poetry, the revised version is superior; but the earliest version is more revealing as autobiography, especially in stanzas omitted from later editions:

> And so, being young and dipt in folly
> I fell in love with melancholy,
> And used to throw my earthly rest
> And quiet all away in jest—
> I could not love except where Death
> Was mingling his with Beauty's breath—

Poe then proceeds to the striking image of "the eternal Condor years" and the resonant climax (preserved in the subsequent editions) in which, at twenty, he declares that he can no longer write poetry for pleasure, but only when he is painfully compelled, when his heart actually "trembles with the strings." That compulsion lasted until his death.

To ——

The bowers whereat, in dreams, I see
   The wantonest singing birds,
Are lips—and all thy melody
   Of lip-begotten words—

Thine eyes, in Heaven of heart enshrined,
   Then desolately fall,
O God! on my funereal mind
   Like starlight on a pall—

Thy heart—*thy* heart!—I wake and sigh,
   And sleep to dream till day
Of the truth that gold can never buy—
   Of the baubles that it may.

Romance

Romance, who loves to nod and sing,
With drowsy head and folded wing,
Among the green leaves as they shake
Far down within some shadowy lake,
To me a painted paroquet
Hath been—a most familiar bird—
Taught me my alphabet to say—
To lisp my very earliest word
While in the wild wood I did lie,
A child—with a most knowing eye.

Of late, eternal Condor years
So shake the very Heaven on high
With tumult as they thunder by,
I have no time for idle cares
Through gazing on the unquiet sky.
And when an hour with calmer wings
Its down upon my spirit flings—
That little time with lyre and rhyme
To while away—forbidden things!
My heart would feel to be a crime
Unless it trembled with the strings.

To the River ——

Fair river! in thy bright, clear flow
 Of crystal, wandering water,
Thou art an emblem of the glow
  Of beauty—the unhidden heart—
  The playful maziness of art
In old Alberto's daughter;

But when within thy wave she looks—
 Which glistens then, and trembles—
Why, then, the prettiest of brooks
 Her worshipper resembles;
For in his heart, as in thy stream,
 Her image deeply lies—
His heart which trembles at the beam
 Of her soul-searching eyes.

TO THE RIVER

Sonnet—To Science

Science! true daughter of Old Time thou art!
    Who alterest all things with thy peering eyes.
Why preyest thou thus upon the poet's heart,
    Vulture, whose wings are dull realities?
How should he love thee? or how deem thee wise,
    Who wouldst not leave him in his wandering
To seek for treasure in the jewelled skies,
    Albeit he soared with an undaunted wing?
Hast thou not dragged Diana from her car?
    And driven the Hamadryad from the wood
To seek a shelter in some happier star?
    Hast thou not torn the Naiad from her flood,
The Elfin from the green grass, and from me
The summer dream beneath the tamarind tree?

To M——

O! I care not that my earthly lot
    Hath little of Earth in it,
That years of love have been forgot
    In the fever of a minute:

I heed not that the desolate
    Are happier, sweet, than I,
But that you meddle with my fate
    Who am a passer by.

It *is* not that my founts of bliss
    Are gushing—strange! with tears—
Or that the thrill of a single kiss
    Hath palsied many years—

'Tis not that the flowers of twenty springs
    Which have wither'd as they rose
Lie dead on my heart-strings
    With the weight of an age of snows.

Not that the grass—O! may it thrive!
    On my grave is growing or grown—
But that, while I am dead yet alive
    I cannot be, lady, alone.

Fairy-land Dim vales—and shadowy floods—
And cloudy-looking woods,
Whose forms we can't discover
For the tears that drip all over!
Huge moons there wax and wane—
Again—again—again—
Every moment of the night—
Forever changing places—
And they put out the star-light
With the breath from their pale faces.
About twelve by the moon-dial,
One more filmy than the rest
(A kind which, upon trial,
They have found to be the best)
Comes down—still down—and down,
With its centre on the crown
Of a mountain's eminence,
While its wide circumference
In easy drapery falls
Over hamlets, over halls,
Wherever they may be—
O'er the strange woods—o'er the sea—
Over spirits on the wing—
Over every drowsy thing—
And buries them up quite
In a labyrinth of light—
And then, how deep!—O, deep!
Is the passion of their sleep.
In the morning they arise,
And their moony covering
Is soaring in the skies,
With the tempests as they toss,
Like—almost anything—
Or a yellow Albatross.
They use that moon no more
For the same end as before—
Videlicet, a tent—
Which I think extravagant:
Its atomies, however,
Into a shower dissever,
Of which those butterflies
Of Earth, who seek the skies,
And so come down again,
(Never-contented things!)
Have brought a specimen
Upon their quivering wings.

FAIRY-LAND

Al Aaraaf

O! nothing earthly save the ray
(Thrown back from flowers) of Beauty's eye,
As in those gardens where the day
Springs from the gems of Circassy—
O! nothing earthly save the thrill
Of melody in woodland rill—
Or (music of the passion-hearted)
Joy's voice so peacefully departed
That like the murmur in the shell,
Its echo dwelleth and will dwell—
Oh, nothing of the dross of ours—
Yet all the beauty—all the flowers
That list our Love, and deck our bowers—
Adorn yon world afar, afar—
The wandering star.

'Twas a sweet time for Nesace—for there
Her world lay lolling on the golden air,
Near four bright suns—a temporary rest—
An oasis in desert of the blest.
Away—away—'mid seas of rays that roll
Empyrean splendor o'er th' unchained soul—
The soul that scarce (the billows are so dense)
Can struggle to its destin'd eminence,—
To distant spheres, from time to time, she rode
And late to ours, the favor'd one of God—
But, now, the ruler of an anchor'd realm,
She throws aside the sceptre—leaves the helm,
And, amid incense and high spiritual hymns,
Laves in quadruple light her angel limbs.

Now happiest, loveliest in yon lovely Earth,
Whence sprang the "Idea of Beauty" into birth,
(Falling in wreaths thro' many a startled star,
Like woman's hair 'mid pearls, until, afar,
It lit on hills Achaian, and there dwelt)
She looked into Infinity—and knelt.
Rich clouds, for canopies, about her curled—
Fit emblems of the model of her world—
Seen but in beauty—not impeding sight
Of other beauty glittering thro' the light—
A wreath that twined each starry form around,
And all the opal'd air in color bound.

     All hurriedly she knelt upon a bed
Of flowers: of lilies such as rear'd the head
On the fair Capo Deucato,[1] and sprang
So eagerly around about to hang
Upon the flying footsteps of—deep pride—
Of her who lov'd a mortal—and so died.[2]
The Sephalica, budding with young bees,
Upreared its purple stem around her knees:—
And gemmy flower, of Trebizond misnam'd[3]—
Inmate of highest stars, where erst it sham'd
All other loveliness:—its honied dew
(The fabled nectar that the heathen knew)
Deliriously sweet, was dropp'd from Heaven,
And fell on gardens of the unforgiven
In Trebizond—and on a sunny flower
So like its own above that, to this hour,
It still remaineth, torturing the bee
With madness, and unwonted reverie:
In Heaven, and all its environs, the leaf
And blossom of the fairy plant in grief
Disconsolate linger—grief that hangs her head,
Repenting follies that full long have fled,
Heaving her white breast to the balmy air,
Like guilty beauty, chasten'd and more fair:
Nyctanthes too, as sacred as the light
She fears to perfume, perfuming the night:
And Clytia, pondering between many a sun,[4]
While pettish tears adown her petals run:
And that aspiring flower that sprang on Earth,[5]
And died, ere scarce exalted into birth,
Bursting its odorous heart in spirit to wing
Its way to Heaven, from garden of a king:
And Valisnerian lotus, thither flown[6]
From struggling with the waters of the Rhone:
And thy most lovely purple perfume, Zante![7]
Isola d'oro!—Fior di Levante!
And the Nelumbo bud that floats for ever
With Indian Cupid down the holy river[8]—
Fair flowers, and fairy! to whose care is given
To bear the Goddess' song, in odors, up to Heaven:[9]

       "Spirit! that dwellest where,
         In the deep sky,
       The terrible and fair,
         In beauty vie!

Beyond the line of blue—
    The boundary of the star
Which turneth at the view
    Of thy barrier and thy bar—
Of the barrier overgone
    By the comets who were cast
From their pride and from their throne
    To be drudges till the last—
To be carriers of fire
    (The red fire of their heart)
With speed that may not tire
    And with pain that shall not part—
Who livest—*that* we know—
    In Eternity—we feel—
But the shadow of whose brow
    What spirit shall reveal?
Tho' the beings whom thy Nesace,
    Thy messenger hath known
Have dream'd for thy Infinity
    A model of their own[10]—
Thy will is done, O God!
    The star hath ridden high
Thro' many a tempest, but she rode
    Beneath thy burning eye;
And here, in thought, to thee—
    In thought that can alone
Ascend thy empire and so be
    A partner of thy throne—
By wingèd Fantasy,[11]
My embassy is given,
Till secrecy shall knowledge be
    In the environs of Heaven."

She ceas'd—and buried then her burning cheek
Abash'd, amid the lilies there, to seek
A shelter from the fervor of His eye;
For the stars trembled at the Deity.
She stirr'd not—breath'd not—for a voice was there
How solemnly pervading the calm air!
A sound of silence on the startled ear
Which dreamy poets name "the music of the sphere."
Ours is a world of words: Quiet we call
"Silence"—which is the merest word of all.
All Nature speaks, and ev'n ideal things
Flap shadowy sounds from visionary wings—

But ah! not so when, thus, in realms on high
The eternal voice of God is passing by,
And the red winds are withering in the sky:—

"What tho' in worlds which sightless cycles run,[12]
Linked to a little system, and one sun—
Where all my love is folly and the crowd
Still think my terrors but the thunder cloud,
The storm, the earthquake, and the ocean-wrath—
(Ah! will they cross me in my angrier path?)
What tho' in worlds which own a single sun
The sands of Time grow dimmer as they run,
Yet thine is my resplendency, so given
To bear my secrets thro' the upper Heaven!
Leave tenantless thy crystal home, and fly,
With all thy train, athwart the moony sky—
Apart—like fire-flies in Sicilian night,[13]
And wing to other worlds another light!
Divulge the secrets of thy embassy
To the proud orbs that twinkle—and so be
To ev'ry heart a barrier and a ban
Lest the stars totter in the guilt of man!"

Up rose the maiden in the yellow night,
The single-moonèd eve!—on Earth we plight
Our faith to one love—and one moon adore—
The birth-place of young Beauty had no more.
As sprang that yellow star from downy hours
Up rose the maiden from her shrine of flowers,
And bent o'er sheeny mountains and dim plain
Her way, but left not yet her Therasaean reign.[14]

PART II

High on a mountain of enamell'd head—
Such as the drowsy shepherd on his bed
Of giant pasturage lying at his ease,
Raising his heavy eyelid, starts and sees
With many a mutter'd "hope to be forgiven"
What time the moon is quadrated in Heaven—
Of rosy head that, towering far away
Into the sunlit ether, caught the ray
Of sunken suns at eve—at noon of night,
While the moon danc'd with the fair stranger light—
Uprear'd upon such height arose a pile

Of gorgeous columns on th' unburthen'd air,
Flashing from Parian marble that twin smile
Far down upon the wave that sparkled there,
And nursled the young mountain in its lair.
Of molten stars their pavement, such as fall
Thro' the ebon air,[15] besilvering the pall
Of their own dissolution, while they die—
Adorning then the dwellings of the sky.
A dome, by linkèd light from Heaven let down,
Sat gently on these columns as a crown—
A window of one circular diamond, there,
Look'd out above into the purple air,
And rays from God shot down that meteor chain
And hallow'd all the beauty twice again,
Save, when, between th' Empyrean and that ring,
Some eager spirit flapp'd his dusky wing.
But on the pillars Seraph eyes have seen
The dimness of this world: that greyish green
That Nature loves the best for Beauty's grave
Lurk'd in each cornice, round each architrave—
And every sculptur'd cherub thereabout
That from his marble dwelling peerèd out,
Seem'd earthly in the shadow of his niche—
Achaian statues in a world so rich!
Friezes from Tadmor and Persepolis[16]—
From Balbec, and the stilly, clear abyss
Of beautiful Gomorrah! O, the wave[17]
Is now upon thee—but too late to save!

Sound loves to revel in a summer night:
Witness the murmur of the grey twilight
That stole upon the ear, in Eyraco,[18]
Of many a wild star-gazer long ago—
That stealeth ever on the ear of him
Who, musing, gazeth on the distance dim,
And sees the darkness coming as a cloud—
Is not its form—its voice—most palpable and loud?[19]

But what is this?—it cometh, and it brings
A music with it—'tis the rush of wings—
A pause—and then a sweeping, falling strain
And Nesace is in her halls again.
From the wild energy of wanton haste
    Her cheeks were flushing, and her lips apart;

And zone that clung around her gentle waist
   Had burst beneath the heaving of her heart.
Within the centre of that hall to breathe,
She paused and panted, Zanthe! all beneath,
The fairy light that kiss'd her golden hair
And long'd to rest, yet could but sparkle there.

   Young flowers were whispering in melody[20]
To happy flowers that night—and tree to tree;
Fountains were gushing music as they fell
In many a star-lit grove, or moon-lit dell;
Yet silence came upon material things—
Fair flowers, bright waterfalls and angel wings—
And sound alone that from the spirit sprang
Bore burthen to the charm the maiden sang:

   " 'Neath the blue-bell or streamer—
     Or tufted wild spray
That keeps, from the dreamer,
     The moonbeam away[21]—
Bright beings! that ponder,
     With half closing eyes,
On the stars which your wonder
     Hath drawn from the skies,
Till they glance thro' the shade, and
     Come down to your brow
Like—eyes of the maiden
     Who calls on you now—
Arise! from your dreaming
     In violet bowers,
To duty beseeming
     These star-litten hours—
And shake from your tresses
     Encumber'd with dew
The breath of those kisses
     That cumber them too—
(O! how, without you, Love!
     Could angels be blest?)
Those kisses of true Love
     That lull'd ye to rest!
Up!—shake from your wing
     Each hindering thing:
The dew of the night—
     It would weigh down your flight
And true love caresses—

AL AARAAF

O, leave them apart!
They are light on the tresses,
　But lead on the heart.

Ligeia! Ligeia!
　My beautiful one!
Whose harshest idea
　Will to melody run,
O! is it thy will
　On the breezes to toss?
Or, capriciously still,
　Like the lone Albatross,[22]
Incumbent on night
　(As she on the air)
To keep watch with delight
　On the harmony there?

Ligeia! wherever
　Thy image may be,
No magic shall sever
　Thy music from thee.
Thou hast bound many eyes
　In a dreamy sleep—
But the strains still arise
　Which *thy* vigilance keep—
The sound of the rain,
　Which leaps down to the flower—
And dances again
　In the rhythm of the shower—
The murmur that springs[23]
　From the growing of grass
Are the music of things—
　But are modell'd, alas!—
Away, then, my dearest,
　Oh! hie thee away
To the springs that lie clearest
　Beneath the moon-ray—
To lone lake that smiles,
　In its dream of deep rest,
At the many star-isles
　That enjewel its breast—
Where wild flowers, creeping,
　Have mingled their shade,
On its margin is sleeping

Full many a maid—
Some have left the cool glade, and
Have slept with the bee[24]—
Arouse them, my maiden,
On moorland and lea—
Go! breathe on their slumber,
All softly in ear,
Thy musical number
They slumbered to hear—
For what can awaken
An angel so soon,
Whose sleep hath been taken
Beneath the cold moon,
As the spell which no slumber
Of witchery may test,
The rhythmical number
Which lull'd him to rest?"

Spirits in wing, and angels to the view,
A thousand seraphs burst th' Empyrean thro',
Young dreams still hovering on their drowsy flight—
Seraphs in all but "Knowledge," the keen light
That fell, refracted, thro' thy bounds, afar,
O Death! from eye of God upon that star:
Sweet was that error—sweeter still that death—
Sweet was that error—even with *us* the breath
Of Science dims the mirror of our joy—
To them 'twere the Simoom, and would destroy—
For what (to them) availeth it to know
That Truth is Falsehood—or that Bliss is Woe?
Sweet was their death—with them to die was rife
With the last ecstasy of satiate life—
Beyond that death no immortality—
But sleep that pondereth and is not "to be"—
And there—oh! may my weary spirit dwell—
Apart from Heaven's Eternity—and yet how far from Hell![25]
What guilty spirit, in what shrubbery dim,
Heard not the stirring summons of that hymn?
But two: they fell: for Heaven no grace imparts
To those who hear not for their beating hearts.
A maiden-angel and her seraph-lover—
O! where (and ye may seek the wide skies over)
Was Love, the blind, near sober Duty known?
Unguided Love hath fallen—'mid "tears of perfect moan."[26]

He was a goodly spirit—he who fell:
A wanderer by moss-y-mantled well—
A gazer on the lights that shine above—
A dreamer in the moonbeam by his love:
What wonder? for each star is eye-like there,
And looks so sweetly down on Beauty's hair—
And they, and ev'ry mossy spring were holy
To his love-haunted heart and melancholy.
The night had found (to him a night of woe)
Upon a mountain crag, young Angelo—
Beetling it bends athwart the solemn sky,
And scowls on starry worlds that down beneath it lie.
Here sat he with his love—his dark eye bent
With eagle gaze along the firmament:
Now turn'd it upon her—but ever then
It trembled to the orb of EARTH again.

"Ianthe, dearest, see—how dim that ray!
How lovely 'tis to look so far away!
She seem'd not thus upon that autumn eve
I left her gorgeous halls—nor mourn'd to leave.
That eve—that eve—I should remember well—
The sun-ray dropp'd in Lemnos, with a spell
On th' arabesque carving of a gilded hall
Wherein I sate, and on the draperied wall—
And on my eyelids—O the heavy light!
How drowsily it weigh'd them into night!
On flowers, before, and mist, and love they ran
With Persian Saadi in his Gulistan:
But O that light!—I slumber'd—Death, the while,
Stole o'er my senses in that lovely isle
So softly that no single silken hair
Awoke that slept—or knew that he was there.

"The last spot of Earth's orb I trod upon
Was a proud temple call'd the Parthenon;[27]
More beauty clung around her column'd wall
Than ev'n thy glowing bosom beats withal,[28]
And when old Time my wing did disenthral
Thence sprang I—as the eagle from his tower,
And years I left behind me in an hour.
What time upon her airy bounds I hung,
One half the garden of her globe was flung
Unrolling as a chart unto my view—

Tenantless cities of the desert too!
Ianthe, beauty crowded on me then,
And half I wish'd to be again of men."

"My Angelo! and why of them to be?
A brighter dwelling-place is here for thee—
And greener fields than in yon world above,
And woman's loveliness—and passionate love."

"But, list, Ianthe! when the air so soft
Fail'd, as my pennon'd spirit leapt aloft,[29]
Perhaps my brain grew dizzy—but the world
I left so late was into chaos hurl'd—
Sprang from her station, on the winds apart.
And roll'd, a flame, the fiery Heaven athwart.
Methought, my sweet one, then I ceased to soar
And fell—not swiftly as I rose before,
But with a downward, tremulous motion thro'
Light, brazen rays, this golden star unto!
Nor long the measure of my falling hours,
For nearest of all stars was thine to ours—
Dread star! that came, amid a night of mirth,
A red Daedalion on the timid Earth."

"We came—and to thy Earth—but not to us
Be given our lady's bidding to discuss:
We came, my love; around, above, below,
Gay fire-fly of the night we come and go,
Nor ask a reason save the angel-nod
She grants to us, as granted by her God—
But, Angelo, than thine grey Time unfurl'd
Never his fairy wing o'er fairier world!
Dim was its little disk, and angel eyes
Alone could see the phantom in the skies,
When first Al Aaraaf knew her course to be
Headlong thitherward o'er the starry sea—
But when its glory swell'd upon the sky,
As glowing Beauty's bust beneath man's eye,
We paused before the heritage of men,
And thy star trembled—as doth Beauty then!"

Thus, in discourse, the lovers whiled away
The night that waned and waned and brought no day.
They fell: for Heaven to them no hope imparts
Who hear not for the beating of their hearts.

44

Notes which the Poet composed
for the preceding Poem

Title] *Al Aaraaf.* A star was discovered by Tycho Brahe which appeared suddenly in the heavens—attained, in a few days, a brilliancy surpassing that of Jupiter—then as suddenly disappeared, and has never been seen since.

1. *On the fair Capo Deucato.* On Santa Maura—olim Deucadia.

2. *Of her who lov'd a mortal—and so died.* Sappho.

3. *And gemmy flower, of Trebizond misnam'd.* This flower is much noticed by Lewenhoeck and Tournefort. The bee, feeding upon its blossom, becomes intoxicated.

4. *And Clytia, pondering between many a sun.* Clytia—the Chrysanthemum Peruvianum, or, to employ a better-known term, the turnsol—which turns continually towards the sun, covers itself, like Peru, the country from which it comes, with dewy clouds which cool and refresh its flowers during the most violent heat of the day.—B. DE ST. PIERRE.

5. *And that aspiring flower that sprang on Earth.* There is cultivated in the king's garden at Paris, a species of serpentine aloes without prickles, whose large and beautiful flower exhales a strong odor of the vanilla, during the time of its expansion, which is very short. It does not blow till towards the month of July—you then perceive it gradually open its petals—expand them—fade and die.—ST. PIERRE.

6. *And Valisnerian lotus, thither flown.* There is found, in the Rhone, a beautiful lily of the Valisnerian kind. Its stem will stretch to the length of three or four feet—thus preserving its head above water in the swellings of the river.

7. *And thy most lovely purple perfume, Zante.* The Hyacinth.

8.   *And the Nelumbo bud that floats for ever*
        With Indian Cupid down the holy river—
It is a fiction of the Indians, that Cupid was first seen floating in one of these down the river Ganges—and that he still loves the cradle of his childhood.

9. *To bear the Goddess' song, in odors, up to Heaven.* And golden vials full of odors, which are the prayers of the saints.—REV. ST. JOHN.

10. *A model of their own.* The Humanitarians held that God was to be understood as having really a human form—*Vide* CLARKE's *Sermons*, vol. i, p. 26, fol. edit.
The drift of Milton's argument leads him to employ language which would appear, at first sight, to verge upon their doctrine; but it would be seen immediately, that he guards himself against the charge of having adopted one of the most ignorant errors of the dark ages of the church.—Dr. SUMNER's *Notes on Milton's Christian Doctrine.*

This opinion, in spite of many testimonies to the contrary, could never have been very general. Andeus, a Syrian of Mesopotamia, was condemned for the opinion, as heretical. He lived in the beginning of the fourth century. His disciples were called Anthropomorphites.— *Vide* Du Pin.

Among Milton's minor poems are these lines:

"Dicite sacrorum presides nemorum Deae, &c.
Quis ille primus cujus ex imagine
Natura solers finxit humanum genus?
Eternus, incorruptus, aequaevus polo,
Unusque et universus, exemplar Dei."

And afterwards—

"Non cui profundum Caecitas lumen dedit
Dircaeus augur vidit hunc alto sinu," &c.

11. *By wingèd Fantasy.*

Fantasy. Seltsamen Tochter Jovis
Seinem Schosskinde,
Der Phantasie.—Goethe.

12. *What tho' in worlds which sightless cycles run.* Sightless— too small to be seen.—Legge.

13. *Apart—like fire-flies in Sicilian night.* I have often noticed a peculiar movement of the fire-flies;—they will collect in a body, and fly off, from a common centre, into innumerable radii.

14. *Her way, but left not yet her Therasaean reign.* Therasaea, or Therasea, the island mentioned by Seneca, which, in a moment, arose from the sea to the eyes of astonished mariners.

PART II

15. *Of molten stars their pavement, such as fall
Thro' the ebon air.*

Some star, which from the ruin'd roof
Of shaked Olympus, by mischance, did fall.—Milton.

16. *Friezes from Tadmor and Persepolis.* Voltaire, in speaking of Persepolis, says, "Je connois bien l'admiration qu'inspirent ces ruines —mais un palais érigé au pied d'une chaîne de rochers stériles, peut-il être un chef-d'œuvre des arts?"

17. *Of beautiful Gomorrah! O, the wave.* Ula Deguisi is the Turkish appellation; but, on its own shores, it is called Bahar Loth, or Almotanah. There were undoubtedly more than two cities engulfed in the "Dead Sea." In the valley of Siddim were five—Admah, Zeboin, Zoar, Sodom and Gomorrah. Stephen of Byzantium mentions eight, and Strabo thirteen (engulfed)—but the last is out of all reason.

It is said [Tacitus, Strabo, Josephus, Daniel of St. Saba, Nau, Maundrell, Troilo, D'Arvieux] that after an excessive drought, the vestiges of columns, walls, &c., are seen above the surface. At *any* season, such remains may be discovered by looking down into the transparent lake, and at such distances as would argue the existence of many settlements in the space now usurped by the "Asphaltites."

18. *That stole upon the ear, in Eyraco.* Eyraco—Chaldea.

19. *Is not its form—its voice—most palpable and loud?* I have often thought I could distinctly hear the sound of the darkness as it stole over the horizon.

20. *Young flowers were whispering in melody.* Fairies use flowers for their charactery.—*Merry Wives of Windsor.*

21. *The moonbeam away.* In Scripture is this passage—"The sun shall not harm thee by day, nor the moon by night." It is perhaps not generally known that the moon, in Egypt, has the effect of producing blindness to those who sleep with the face exposed to its rays, to which circumstance the passage evidently alludes.

22. *Like the lone Albatross.* The albatross is said to sleep on the wing.

23. *The murmur that springs.* I met with this idea in an old English tale, which I am now unable to obtain, and quote from memory: —"The verie essence and, as it were, springeheade and origine of all musiche is the verie plesaunte sounde which the trees of the forest do make when they growe."

24. *Have slept with the bee.* The wild bee will not sleep in the shade if there be moonlight.

The rhyme in this verse, as in one about sixty lines before, has an appearance of affectation. It is, however, imitated from Sir W. Scott, or rather from Claude Halcro—in whose mouth I admired its effect:

> "Oh! were there an island
> Though ever so wild,
> Where woman might smile, and
> No man be beguiled," &c.

25. *Apart from Heaven's Eternity—and yet how far from Hell!* With the Arabians there is a medium between Heaven and Hell, where men suffer no punishment, but yet do not attain that tranquil and even happiness which they suppose to be characteristic of heavenly enjoyment.

> Un no rompido sueño,
> Un die puro, alegre, libre quiero; . . .
> Libre de amor, de zelo,
> De odio, de esperanzas, de recelo.
>   LUIS PONCE DE LEÓN.

Sorrow is not excluded from "Al Aaraaf," but it is that sorrow which the living love to cherish for the dead, and which, in some minds, resembles the delirium of opium. The passionate excitement of

Love and the buoyancy of spirit attendant upon intoxication are its less holy pleasures—the price of which, to those souls who make choice of "Al Aaraaf" as their residence after life, is final death and annihilation.

26. *Unguided Love hath fallen—'mid "tears of perfect moan."*

There be tears of perfect moan

Wept for thee in Helicon.—MILTON.

27. *Was a proud temple call'd the Parthenon.* It was entire in 1687 —the most elevated spot in Athens.

28. *Than ev'n thy glowing bosom beats withal.*

Shadowing more beauty in their airy brows

Than have the white breasts of the Queen of Love.—MARLOWE.

29. *Fail'd as my pennon'd spirit leapt aloft.* Pennon—for pinion. —MILTON.

The Poems of Edgar Allan Poe

III

THE PURPOSE OF POETRY

[AN ESSAY]

AT TWENTY-TWO Poe was already on the defensive. He had failed as a student, a soldier, and, in his relations with his foster-father, as a son; he was mortally afraid of failing as a poet. Two volumes of his poetry had been published without acclaim; a third, the *Poems* of 1831, began with a partly self-apologetic, partly supercilious preface. Using the disguise of a letter to "Dear B—," who may have been Poe's publisher Elam Bliss, Poe maintained that a poet is his own best critic; that Milton probably preferred the lyrical "Comus" to the epical "Paradise Lost"; that Coleridge, though a giant, was prone to err; and that he had no faith in Wordsworth, a dull "metaphysical" poet who wore away his youth in contemplation "with the end of poetizing in his manhood." Pitting himself against the great reputations of the past, how was the young poet ever to succeed? Even the present was too busily competitive. The New England writers were appreciated by the public and applauded by the critics. Names from abroad were still more alluring; title-pages that carried the "mystic characters which spell London, Paris or Geneva are precisely so many letters of recommendation."

But if, at twenty-two, Poe was fearful of a competitive world, he was also planning his escape from it. As a poet, he would devote himself to sensation, to "an elevating excitement," the intoxication of the word. Poetry should not instruct; it should be "purposeless," pure in its impressionism. "Poetry, above all things, is a beautiful painting whose tints, to minute inspection, are confusion worse confounded, but start boldly out to the cursory glance of the connoisseur."

Here Poe announced his creed. It was, to a great extent, Coleridge's. Poe's often quoted dictum, "A poem, in my opinion, is opposed to a work of science by having for its *immediate* object pleasure, not truth," first appeared, almost word for word, in Chapter XIV of Coleridge's *Biographia Literaria*. But Poe extended the implications. For him the enchantment of poetry was its *indefinite* pleasure rather than definite meaning, and he progressed rapidly toward a verbal music in which sound all but triumphed over sense.

The Purpose of Poetry

DEAR B——,

Believing only a portion of my former volume to be worthy of a second edition—that small portion I thought it as well to include in the present book as to republish by itself. I have, therefore, herein combined "Al Aaraaf" and "Tamerlane" with other Poems hitherto unprinted. Nor have I hesitated to insert from the "Minor Poems" now omitted whole lines, and even passages, to the end that, being placed in a fairer light, and the trash shaken from them in which they were imbedded, they may have some chance of being seen by posterity.

It has been said, that a good critique on a poem may be written by one who is no poet himself. This, according to *your* idea and *mine* of poetry, I feel to be false—the less poetical the critic, the less just the critique, and the converse. On this account, and because there are but few B——s in the world, I would be as much ashamed of the world's good opinion as proud of your own. Another than yourself might here observe, "Shakespeare is in possession of the world's good opinion, and yet Shakespeare is the greatest of poets. It appears then that the world judge correctly; why should you be ashamed of their favorable judgment?" The difficulty lies in the interpretation of the word "judgment" or "opinion." The opinion is the world's, truly, but it may be called theirs as a man would call a book his, having bought it: he did not write the book, but it is his; they did not originate the opinion, but it is theirs. A fool, for example, thinks Shakespeare a great poet—yet the fool has never read Shakespeare. But the fool's neighbor, who is a step higher on the Andes of the mind, whose head (that is to say, his more exalted thought) is too far above the fool to be seen or understood, but whose feet (by which I mean his everyday actions) are sufficiently near to be discerned, and by means of which that superiority is ascertained, which *but* for them would never have been discovered —this neighbor asserts that Shakespeare is a great poet—the fool believes him, and it is henceforward his *opinion*. This neighbor's own opinion has, in like manner, been adopted from one above *him*, and so, ascendingly, to a few gifted individuals, who kneel around the summit, beholding, face to face, the master spirit who stands upon the pinnacle.

You are aware of the great barrier in the path of an American writer. He is read, if at all, in preference to the combined and established wit of the world. I say established: for it is with literature as with law or empire—an established name is an estate in tenure, or a throne in possession. Besides, one might suppose that books, like their authors, improve by travel—their having crossed the sea is, with us, so great a distinction. Our antiquaries abandon time for distance: our very fops glance from the binding to the bottom of the title-page, where the mystic characters which spell London, Paris, or Geneva, are precisely so many letters of recommendation.

I mentioned just now a vulgar error as regards criticism. I think the notion that no poet can form a correct estimate of his own writings is another. I remarked before, that in proportion to the poetical talent would be the justice of a critique upon poetry. Therefore, a bad poet would, I grant, make a false critique, and his self-love would infallibly bias his little judgment in his favor; but a poet, who is indeed a poet, could not, I think, fail of making a just critique. Whatever should be deducted on the score of self-love, might be replaced on account of his intimate acquaintance with the subject; in short, we have more instances of false criticism, than of just, where one's own writings are the test, simply because we have more bad poets than good. There are of course many objections to what I say: Milton is a great example of the contrary; but his opinion with respect to the "Paradise Regained" is by no means fairly ascertained. By what trivial circumstances men are often led to assert what they do not really believe! Perhaps an inadvertent word has descended to posterity. But, in fact, the "Paradise Regained" is little, if at all, inferior to the "Paradise Lost," and is only supposed so to be, because men do not like epics, whatever they may say to the contrary, and reading those of Milton in their natural order, are too much wearied with the first to derive any pleasure from the second.

I dare say Milton preferred "Comus" to either—if so, justly.

As I am speaking of poetry, it will not be amiss to touch slightly upon the most singular heresy in its modern history—the heresy of what is called, very foolishly, the "Lake School." Some years ago I might have been induced, by an occasion like the present, to attempt a formal refutation of their doctrine; at present it would be a work of supererogation. The wise must bow to the wisdom of such men as Coleridge and Southey, but being wise, have laughed at poetical theories so prosaically exemplified.

Aristotle, with singular assurance, has declared poetry the most philosophical of all writing*—but it required a Wordsworth to pronounce it most metaphysical. He seems to think that the end of poetry is, or should be, instruction—yet it is a truism that the end of our existence is happiness; if so, the end of every separate part of our existence—everything connected with our existence—should be still happiness. Therefore the end of instruction should be happiness; and happiness is another name for pleasure;—therefore the end of instruction should be pleasure; yet we see the above-mentioned opinion implies precisely the reverse.

---

*Σπουδαιότατον καὶ φιλοσοφικώτατον γένος.

To proceed: *Cœteris paribus,* he who pleases is of more importance to his fellow men than he who instructs, since utility is happiness, and pleasure is the end already obtained which instruction is merely the means of obtaining.

I see no reason, then, why our metaphysical poets should plume themselves so much on the utility of their works, unless indeed they refer to instruction with eternity in view: in which case, sincere respect for their piety would not allow me to express my contempt for their judgment; contempt which it would be difficult to conceal since their writings are professedly to be understood by the few, and it is the many who stand in need of salvation. In such case I should no doubt be tempted to think of the devil in Melmoth, who labors indefatigably through three octavo volumes to accomplish the destruction of one or two souls, while any common devil would have demolished one or two thousand.

Against the subtleties which would make poetry a study—not a passion—it becomes the metaphysician to reason, but the poet to protest. Yet Wordsworth and Coleridge are men in years; the one imbued in contemplation from childhood, the other a giant in intellect and learning. The diffidence, then, with which I venture to dispute their authority would be overwhelming, did not I feel, from the bottom of my heart, that learning has little to do with the imagination—intellect with the passions—or age with poetry.

> Trifles, like straws, upon the surface flow;
> He who would search for pearls must dive below,

are lines which have done much mischief. As regards the greater truths, men oftener err by seeking them at the bottom than at the top; the depth lies in the huge abysses where wisdom is sought—not in the palpable palaces where she is found. The ancients were not always right in hiding the goddess in a well; witness the light which Bacon has thrown upon philosophy: witness the principles of our divine faith —that moral mechanism by which the simplicity of a child may overbalance the wisdom of a man.

Poetry, above all things, is a beautiful painting whose tints, to minute inspection, are confusion worse confounded, but start boldly out to the cursory glance of the connoisseur.

We see an instance of Coleridge's liability to err in his "Biographia Literaria"—professedly his literary life and opinions, but, in fact, a treatise *de omni scibili et quibusdam aliis.* He goes wrong by reason of his very profundity, and of his error we have a natural type in the contemplation of a star. He who regards it directly and intensely sees, it is true, the star, but it is the star without a ray—while he who surveys it less inquisitively is conscious of all for which the star is useful to us below—its brilliance and its beauty.

As to Wordsworth, I have no faith in him. That he had, in youth, the feelings of a poet, I believe—for there are glimpses of extreme delicacy in his writings (and delicacy is the poet's own kingdom—his *el dorado*)—but they have the appearance of a better day recollected; and glimpses, at best, are little evidence of present poetic fire—we know that a few straggling flowers spring up daily in the crevices of the avalanche.

He was to blame in wearing away his youth in contemplation with the end of poetizing in his manhood. With the increase of his judgment, the light which should make it apparent has faded away. His judgment consequently is too correct. This may not be understood, but the old Goths of Germany would have understood it, who used to debate matters of importance to their State twice, once when drunk, and once when sober—sober that they might not be deficient in formality—drunk lest they should be destitute of vigor.

The long wordy discussions by which he tries to reason us into admiration of his poetry, speak very little in his favor. They are full of such assertions as this (I have opened one of his volumes at random): "Of genius the only proof is the act of doing well what is worthy to be done, and what was never done before." Indeed! then it follows that in doing what is *un*worthy to be done, or what *has* been done before, no genius can be evinced: yet the picking of pockets is an unworthy act, pockets have been picked time immemorial, and Barrington, the pickpocket, in point of genius would have thought hard of a comparison with William Wordsworth, the poet.

Again—in estimating the merit of certain poems, whether they be Ossian's or M'Pherson's, can surely be of little consequence, yet, in order to prove their worthlessness, Mr. W. has expended many pages in the controversy. *Tantœne animis?* Can great minds descend to such absurdity? But worse still: that he may beat down every argument in favor of these poems, he triumphantly drags forward a passage, in his abomination of which he expects the reader to sympathize. It is the beginning of the epic poem, "Temora." "The blue waves of Ullin roll in light; the green hills are covered with day; trees shake their dusky heads in the breeze." And this—this gorgeous, yet simple imagery— where all is alive and panting with immortality—than which earth has nothing more grand, nor paradise more beautiful—this—William Wordsworth, the author of "Peter Bell," has *selected* to dignify with his supreme contempt. We shall see what better he, in his own person, has to offer. Imprimis:

> And now she's at the pony's head,
> And now she's at the pony's tail,
> On that side now, and now on this,
> And almost stifled her with bliss—
> A few sad tears does Betty shed,
> She pats the pony, where or when
> She knows not, happy Betty Fry!
> O Johnny, never mind the Doctor!

Secondly:

> The dew was falling fast, the—stars began to blink
> I heard a voice, it said—Drink, pretty creature, drink;
> And looking o'er the edge, be—fore me I espied
> A snow-white mountain lamb with a—maiden at its side.
> No other sheep were near, the lamb was all alone,
> And by a slender cord was—tethered to a stone.

Now, we have no doubt this is all true; we *will* believe it—indeed we will, Mr. W. Is it sympathy for the sheep you wish to excite? I love a sheep from the bottom of my heart.

But there *are* occasions, dear B——, there are occasions when even Wordsworth is reasonable. Even Stamboul, it is said, shall have an end, and the most unlucky blunders must come to a conclusion. Here is an extract from his preface:—

"Those who have been accustomed to the phraseology of modern writers, if they persist in reading this book to a conclusion" *(impossible!)* "will, no doubt, have to struggle with feelings of awkwardness" (ha! ha! ha!); "they will look round for poetry" (ha! ha! ha! ha!), "and will be induced to inquire by what species of courtesy these attempts have been permitted to assume that title." Ha! ha! ha! ha! ha!

Yet let not Mr. W. despair, he has given immortality to a wagon and the bee, Sophocles has eternalized a sore toe, and dignified a tragedy with a chorus of turkeys.

Of Coleridge I cannot speak but with reverence. His towering intellect! his gigantic power! To use an author quoted by himself, "J'ai trouvé souvent que la plupart des sectes ont raison dans une bonne partie de ce qu'elles avancent, mais non pas en ce qu'elles nient"; and, to employ his own language, he has imprisoned his own conceptions by the barrier he had erected against those of others. It is lamentable to think that such a mind should be buried in metaphysics, and, like the Nyctanthes, waste its perfume upon the night alone. In reading that man's poetry I tremble like one who stands upon a volcano, conscious, from the very darkness bursting from the crater, of the fire and the light that are weltering below.

What is Poetry? Poetry! That Proteus-like idea, with as many appellations as the nine-titled Corcyra! Give me, I demanded of a scholar some time ago, give me a definition of Poetry. "Très volontiers"—and he proceeded to his library, brought me a Dr. Johnson, and overwhelmed me with a definition. Shade of the immortal Shakespeare! I imagined to myself the scowl of your spiritual eye upon the profanity of that scurrilous Ursa Major. Think of poetry, dear B——, think of the Tempest—the Midsummer Night's Dream—Prospero— that is airy and fairy-like, and then of all that is hideous and unwieldy: think of his huge bulk, the Elephant! and then—and then think of the Tempest—the Midsummer Night's Dream—Prospero— Oberon—and Titania!

A poem, in my opinion, is opposed to a work of science by having for its *immediate* object, pleasure, not truth: to romance, by having for its object an *indefinite* instead of a *definite* pleasure, being a poem only so far as this object is attained: romance presenting perceptible images with definite, poetry with *in*definite sensations, to which end music is an *essential*, since the comprehension of sweet sound is our most indefinite conception. Music, when combined with a pleasurable idea, is poetry: music, without the idea, is simply music: the idea, without the music, is prose from its very definiteness.

What was meant by the invective against "him who had no music in his soul"?

To sum up this long rigmarole, I have, dear B——, what you no doubt perceive, for the metaphysical poets, *as* poets, the most sovereign contempt. That they have followers proves nothing—

> No Indian prince has to his palace
> More followers than a thief to the gallows.

The Poems of Edgar Allan Poe

IV

POEMS ADDED IN THE EDITION OF 1831

POE'S THIRD VOLUME, published in 1831, was severely entitled *Poems*. It contained a prefatory "Letter to B——," and it is thought that the otherwise unidentified "B" may have been the book's publisher, Elam Bliss. The letter (see page 51) is a curious hodge-podge of arrogance and rationalization, echoes from Coleridge and special pleading; but it is the poetry which holds us.

Besides a further revision of "Tamerlane" and other earlier pieces, the 1831 volume contained six new poems, among which are the very best of Poe: the unforgettable lyric "To Helen," every line of which combines pure music and powerful suggestion; "Israfel," in which the angel "who has the sweetest voice of all God's creatures" is the uplifted spirit of Poe, "whose heart-strings were a lute"; "The Valley of Unrest," with its personal evocation of mystery and brooding sorrow; "The City in the Sea," a conception of grandeur and magnificent sound.

The idea of "The City in the Sea" can be found in other literatures, in Uhland's "Die verlorene Kirche" and his "Das versunkene Kloster," in Hauptmann's "Die versunkene Glocke," and in the legend of the sunken city of Ys. But it may not be too fantastic to surmise that Poe's picture of the toppled spires and towers and Babylon-like walls may have been a dream of the downfall of New York, the city in which the poet was so miserable and in which Death had "reared himself a throne."

> And when, amid no earthly moans,
> Down, down that town shall settle hence,
> Hell, rising from a thousand thrones,
> Shall do it reverence.

Is this a weird flash of the poet's imagination or, for all its disguise, a wishful prophecy?

The Valley of Unrest

Once it smiled a silent dell
Where the people did not dwell;
They had gone unto the wars,
Trusting to the mild-eyed stars,
Nightly, from their azure towers,
To keep watch above the flowers,
In the midst of which all day
The red sunlight lazily lay.
Now each visitor shall confess
The sad valley's restlessness.
Nothing there is motionless—
Nothing save the airs that brood
Over the magic solitude.
Ah, by no wind are stirred those trees
That palpitate like the chill seas
Around the misty Hebrides!
Ah, by no wind those clouds are driven
That rustle through the unquiet Heaven
Uneasily, from morn till even,
Over the violets there that lie
In myriad types of the human eye—
Over the lilies there that wave
And weep above a nameless grave!
They wave:—from out their fragrant tops
Eternal dews come down in drops.
They weep:—from off their delicate stems
Perennial tears descend in gems.

To Helen   Helen, thy beauty is to me
                  Like those Nicean barks of yore,
               That gently, o'er a perfumed sea,
                  The weary, wayworn wanderer bore
                  To his own native shore.

               On desperate seas long wont to roam,
                  Thy hyacinth hair, thy classic face,
               Thy Naiad airs have brought me home
                  To the glory that was Greece
               And the grandeur that was Rome.

               Lo! in yon brilliant window-niche
                  How statue-like I see thee stand,
                  The agate lamp within thy hand!
               Ah, Psyche, from the regions which
                  Are Holy Land!

TO HELEN

Israfel In Heaven a spirit doth dwell
                  "Whose heart-strings are a lute";
              None sing so wildly well
              As the angel Israfel,
              And the giddy stars (so legends tell),
              Ceasing their hymns, attend the spell
                  Of his voice, all mute.

              Tottering above
                  In her highest noon,
                  The enamored moon
              Blushes with love,
                  While, to listen, the red levin
                  (With the rapid Pleiads, even,
                  Which were seven,)
                  Pauses in Heaven.

              And they say (the starry choir
                  And the other listening things)
              That Israfeli's fire
              Is owing to that lyre
                  By which he sits and sings—
              The trembling living wire
                  Of those unusual strings.

              But the skies that angel trod,
                  Where deep thoughts are a duty—
              Where Love's a grown-up God—
                  Where the Houri glances are
              Imbued with all the beauty
                  Which we worship in a star.

              Therefore thou art not wrong,
                  Israfeli, who despisest
              An unimpassioned song;
              To thee the laurels belong,
                  Best bard, because the wisest!
              Merrily live, and long!

              The ecstasies above
                  With thy burning measures suit—
              Thy grief, thy joy, thy hate, thy love,
                  With the fervor of thy lute—
                  Well may the stars be mute!

Yes, Heaven is thine; but this
  Is a world of sweets and sours;
  Our flowers are merely—flowers,
And the shadow of thy perfect bliss
  Is the sunshine of ours.

If I could dwell
Where Israfel
  Hath dwelt, and he where I,
He might not sing so wildly well
  A mortal melody,
While a bolder note than this might swell
  From my lyre within the sky.

ISRAFEL

The City in the Sea

Lo! Death has reared himself a throne
In a strange city lying alone
Far down within the dim West,
Where the good and the bad and the worst and the best
Have gone to their eternal rest.
There shrines and palaces and towers
(Time-eaten towers that tremble not!)
Resemble nothing that is ours.
Around, by lifting winds forgot,
Resignedly beneath the sky
The melancholy waters lie.

No rays from the holy heaven come down
On the long night-time of that town;
But light from out the lurid sea
Streams up the turrets silently—
Gleams up the pinnacles far and free—
Up domes—up spires—up kingly halls—
Up fanes—up Babylon-like walls—
Up shadowy long-forgotten bowers
Of sculptured ivy and stone flowers—
Up many and many a marvellous shrine
Whose wreathèd friezes intertwine
The viol, the violet, and the vine.
Resignedly beneath the sky
The melancholy waters lie.
So blend the turrets and shadows there
That all seem pendulous in air,
While from a proud tower in the town
Death looks gigantically down.

There open fanes and gaping graves
Yawn level with the luminous waves;
But not the riches there that lie
In each idol's diamond eye—
Not the gaily-jewelled dead
Tempt the waters from their bed;
For no ripples curl, alas!
Along that wilderness of glass—
No swellings tell that winds may be
Upon some far-off happier sea—
No heavings hint that winds have been
On seas less hideously serene.

But lo, a stir is in the air!
The wave—there is a movement there!
As if the towers had thrust aside,
In slightly sinking, the dull tide—
As if their tops had feebly given
A void within the filmy Heaven.
The waves have now a redder glow—
The hours are breathing faint and low—
And when, amid no earthly moans,
Down, down that town shall settle hence,
Hell, rising from a thousand thrones,
Shall do it reverence.

THE CITY IN THE SEA

The Sleeper At midnight, in the month of June,
I stand beneath the mystic moon.
An opiate vapor, dewy, dim,
Exhales from out her golden rim,
And, softly dripping, drop by drop,
Upon the quiet mountain top,
Steals drowsily and musically
Into the universal valley.
The rosemary nods upon the grave;
The lily lolls upon the wave;
Wrapping the fog about its breast,
The ruin molders into rest;
Looking like Lethe, see! the lake
A conscious slumber seems to take,
And would not, for the world, awake.
All Beauty sleeps!—and lo! where lies
Irene, with her Destinies!

O, lady bright! can it be right—
This window open to the night?
The wanton airs, from the tree-top,
Laughingly through the lattice drop—
The bodiless airs, a wizard rout,
Flit through thy chamber in and out,
And wave the curtain canopy
So fitfully—so fearfully—
Above the closed and fringèd lid
'Neath which thy slumb'ring soul lies hid,
That, o'er the floor and down the wall,
Like ghosts the shadows rise and fall!
Oh, lady dear, hast thou no fear?
Why and what art thou dreaming here?
Sure thou art come o'er far-off seas,
A wonder to these garden trees!
Strange is thy pallor! strange thy dress,
Strange, above all, thy length of tress,
And this all solemn silentness!

The lady sleeps! Oh, may her sleep,
Which is enduring, so be deep!
Heaven have her in its sacred keep!
This chamber changed for one more holy,
This bed for one more melancholy,
I pray to God that she may lie
For ever with unopened eye,
While the pale sheeted ghosts go by!

My love, she sleeps! Oh, may her sleep
As it is lasting, so be deep!
Soft may the worms about her creep!
Far in the forest, dim and old,
For her may some tall vault unfold—
Some vault that oft has flung its black
And wingèd panels fluttering back,
Triumphant, o'er the crested palls,
Of her grand family funerals—
Some sepulchre, remote, alone,
Against whose portal she hath thrown,
In childhood, many an idle stone—
Some tomb from out whose sounding door
She ne'er shall force an echo more,
Thrilling to think, poor child of sin!
It was the dead who groaned within.

THE SLEEPER

Lenore

Ah, broken is the golden bowl! the spirit flown forever!
Let the bell toll!—a saintly soul floats on the Stygian river;
And, Guy de Vere, hast *thou* no tear?—weep now or nevermore!
See! on yon drear and rigid bier low lies thy love, Lenore!
Come! let the burial rite be read—the funeral song be sung!—
An anthem for the queenliest dead that ever died so young—
A dirge for her the doubly dead in that she died so young.

"Wretches! ye loved her for her wealth and hated her for her pride,
And when she fell in feeble health, ye blessed her—that she died!
How *shall* the ritual, then, be read?—the requiem how be sung
By you—by yours, the evil eye,—by yours, the slanderous tongue
That did to death the innocence that died, and died so young?"

Peccavimus; but rave not thus! and let a Sabbath song
Go up to God so solemnly the dead may feel no wrong.
The sweet Lenore hath "gone before," with Hope, that flew beside,
Leaving thee wild for the dear child that should have been thy bride—
For her, the fair and *debonair*, that now so lowly lies,
The life upon her yellow hair but not within her eyes—
The life still there, upon her hair—the death upon her eyes.

  "Avaunt! avaunt! from fiends below, the indignant ghost is riven—
From Hell unto a high estate far up within the Heaven—
From grief and groan, to a golden throne, beside the King of Heaven!
Let no bell toll, then,—lest her soul, amid its hallowed mirth,
Should catch the note as it doth float up from the damnèd Earth!
And I!—to-night my heart is light!—no dirge will I upraise,
But waft the angel on her flight with a Paean of old days!"

The Poems of Edgar Allan Poe

V

THE POETIC PRINCIPLE

[AN ESSAY]

"THE POETIC PRINCIPLE," published in the *Home Journal* in 1850, is an expansion of the critical canons laid down, almost twenty years earlier, in the letter to "B" ———, canons to which Poe, as George Edward Woodberry wrote, "submitted the more easily because they were consonant with his own genius."

It is obvious that "The Poetic Principle" was prepared as a lecture. The spotty generalities, the superficial disposals, the "popular" tone, most of all the choice of quoted poems—Shelley's "Indian Serenade," Willis's maudlin "The shadows lay along Broadway," Longfellow's "The day is done," Bryant's "June," Pinkney's "Health," Moore's "Come, rest in my bosom," Hood's "Fair Ines" and the same author's "Bridge of Sighs," Byron's "Though the day of my destiny's over," Tennyson's "Tears, idle tears," Motherwell's "The Song of the Cavalier"—this oddly assorted assembly of recitation pieces makes it plain that "The Poetic Principle" was primarily addressed to a listening audience rather than to a reading public.

Yet here again Poe tried to pronounce what he believed to be the "true function" of poetry—a function which, unless incidentally, had "no concern whatever either with Duty or with Truth." Devoted to a worship of abstract beauty, Poe stated and restated the theme with continual variations. "An immortal instinct, deep within the spirit of man, is thus, plainly, a sense of the Beautiful. . . . We have still a thirst unquenchable. . . . This thirst belongs to the immortality of Man. It is at once a consequence and an indication of his perennial existence. It is the desire of the moth for the star. It is no mere appreciation of the Beauty before us—but a wild effort to reach the Beauty above." "There cannot exist any work more thoroughly dignified, more supremely noble, than the poem—the poem *per se*—this poem which is a poem and nothing more—this poem written solely for the poem's sake."

Thus Poe, with a minimum of rationalism, could turn from Truth, "which is the satisfaction of the Reason," to Passion, "which is the excitement of the Heart" and to Beauty, "which is not only the province of the poem, but the elevation of the soul."

The Poetic Principle

IN SPEAKING of the Poetic Principle, I have no design to be either thorough or profound. While discussing, very much at random, the essentiality of what we call Poetry, my principal purpose will be to cite for consideration, some few of those minor English or American poems which best suit my own taste, or which, upon my own fancy, have left the most definite impression. By "minor poems" I mean, of course, poems of little length. And here, in the beginning, permit me to say a few words in regard to a somewhat peculiar principle, which, whether rightfully or wrongfully, has always had its influence in my own critical estimate of the poem. I hold that a long poem does not exist. I maintain that the phrase, "a long poem," is simply a flat contradiction in terms.

I need scarcely observe that a poem deserves its title only inasmuch as it excites, by elevating the soul. The value of the poem is in the ratio of this elevating excitement. But all excitements are, through a psychal necessity, transient. That degree of excitement which would entitle a poem to be so called at all, cannot be sustained throughout a composition of any great length. After the lapse of half an hour, at the very utmost, it flags—fails—a revulsion ensues—and then the poem is, in effect, and in fact, no longer such.

There are, no doubt, many who have found difficulty in reconciling the critical dictum that the "Paradise Lost" is to be devoutly admired throughout, with the absolute impossibility of maintaining for it, during perusal, the amount of enthusiasm which that critical dictum would demand. This great work, in fact, is to be regarded as poetical, only when, losing sight of that vital requisite in all works of Art, Unity, we view it merely as a series of minor poems. If, to preserve its Unity—its totality of effect or impression—we read it (as would be necessary) at a single sitting, the result is but a constant alternation of excitement and depression. After a passage of what we feel to be true poetry, there follows, inevitably, a passage of platitude which no critical prejudgment can force us to admire; but if, upon completing the work, we read it again; omitting the first book—that is to say, commencing with the second—we shall be surprised at now finding that admirable which we before condemned—that damnable which we had previously so much admired. It follows from all this that the ultimate, aggregate, or absolute effect of even the best epic under the sun, is a nullity:—and this is precisely the fact.

In regard to the Iliad, we have, if not positive proof, at least very good reason, for believing it intended as a series of lyrics; but, granting the epic intention, I can say only that the work is based in an imperfect sense of Art. The modern epic is of the supposititious ancient model, but an inconsiderate and blindfold imitation. But the day of these artistic anomalies is over. If, at any time, any very long poem *were* popular in reality—which I doubt—it is at least clear that no very long poem will ever be popular again.

That the extent of a poetical work is, *ceteris paribus*, the measure of its merit, seems undoubtedly, when we thus state it, a proposition sufficiently absurd—yet we are indebted for it to the quarterly Reviews. Surely there can be nothing in mere *size*, abstractly considered —there can be nothing in mere *bulk*, so far as a volume is concerned, which has so continuously elicited admiration from these saturnine pamphlets! A mountain, to be sure, by the mere sentiment of physical magnitude which it conveys *does* impress us with a sense of the sublime—but no man is impressed after *this* fashion by the material grandeur of even "The Columbiad." Even the Quarterlies have not instructed us to be so impressed by it. *As yet,* they have not *insisted* on our estimating Lamartine by the cubic foot, or Pollock by the pound— but what else are we to *infer* from their continual prating about "sustained effort"? If, by "sustained effort," any little gentleman has accomplished an epic, let us frankly commend him for the effort—if this indeed be a thing commendable,—but let us forbear praising the epic on the effort's account. It is to be hoped that common-sense, in the time to come, will prefer deciding upon a work of Art, rather by the impression it makes—by the effect it produces—than by the time it took to impress the effect, or by the amount of "sustained effort" which had been found necessary in effecting the impression. The fact is, that perseverance is one thing and genius quite another—nor can all the Quarterlies in Christendom confound them. By-and-by, this proposition, with many which I have been just urging, will be received as self-evident. In the meantime, by being generally condemned as falsities, they will not be essentially damaged as truths.

On the other hand, it is clear that a poem may be improperly brief. Undue brevity degenerates into mere epigrammatism. A *very* short poem, while now and then producing a brilliant or vivid, never produces a profound or enduring, effect. There must be the steady pressing down of the stamp upon the wax. De Béranger has wrought innumerable things, pungent and spirit-stirring; but, in general, they have been too imponderous to stamp themselves deeply into the public attention; and thus, as so many feathers of fancy, have been blown aloft only to be whistled down the wind.

A remarkable instance of the effect of undue brevity in depressing a poem—in keeping it out of the popular view—is afforded by the following exquisite little Serenade:

> I arise from dreams of thee
> In the first sweet sleep of night,
> When the winds are breathing low,
> And the stars are shining bright.

I arise from dreams of thee,
     And a spirit in my feet
Has led me—who knows how?—
     To thy chamber-window, sweet.

The wandering airs they faint
     On the dark, the silent stream—
The champak odors fail
     Like sweet thoughts in a dream;
The nightingale's complaint,
     It dies upon her heart,
As I must die on thine,
     Oh, beloved as thou art!

Oh, lift me from the grass!
     I die, I faint, I fail!
Let thy love in kisses rain
     On my lips and eyelids pale.
My cheek is cold and white, alas!
     My heart beats loud and fast;
Oh, press it close to thine again,
     Where it will break at last!

Very few, perhaps, are familiar with these lines—yet no less a poet than Shelley is their author. Their warm, yet delicate and ethereal imagination will be appreciated by all—but by none so thoroughly as by him who has himself arisen from sweet dreams of one beloved, to bathe in the aromatic air of a southern midsummer night.

One of the finest poems by Willis—the very best, in my opinion, which he has ever written—has, no doubt, through this same defect of undue brevity, been kept back from its proper position, not less in the critical than in the popular view.

The shadows lay along Broadway,
     'T was near the twilight-tide—
And slowly there a lady fair
     Was walking in her pride.
Alone walk'd she; but, viewlessly,
     Walk'd spirits at her side.

Peace charm'd the street beneath her feet,
     And Honor charm'd the air;
And all astir looked kind on her,
     And call'd her good as fair—
For all God ever gave to her,
     She kept with chary care.

She kept with care her beauties rare
   From lovers warm and true—
For her heart was cold to all but gold,
   And the rich came not to woo—
But honored well are charms to sell
   If priests the selling do.

Now walking there was one more fair—
   A slight girl, lily-pale;
And she had unseen company
   To make the spirit quail—
'Twixt Want and Scorn she walk'd forlorn.
   And nothing could avail.

No mercy now can clear her brow
   For this world's peace to pray;
For, as love's wild prayer dissolved in air,
   Her woman's heart gave way!—
But the sin forgiven by Christ in Heaven
   By man is cursed alway!

In this composition we find it difficult to recognize the Willis who has written so many mere "verses of society." The lines are not only richly ideal, but full of energy; while they breathe an earnestness—an evident sincerity of sentiment—for which we look in vain throughout all the other works of this author.

While the epic mania—while the idea that, to merit in poetry, prolixity is indispensable—has, for some years past, been gradually dying out of the public mind, by mere dint of its own absurdity, we find it succeeded by a heresy too palpably false to be long tolerated, but one which, in the brief period it has already endured, may be said to have accomplished more in the corruption of our Poetical Literature than all its other enemies combined. I allude to the heresy of "The Didactic." It has been assumed, tacitly and avowedly, directly and indirectly, that the ultimate object of all Poetry is Truth. Every poem, it is said, should inculcate a moral; and by this moral is the poetical merit of the work to be adjudged. We Americans especially have patronized this happy idea; and we Bostonians, very especially, have developed it in full. We have taken it into our heads that to write a poem simply for the poem's sake, and to acknowledge such to have been our design, would be to confess ourselves radically wanting in the true Poetic dignity and force:—but the simple fact is, that, would we but permit ourselves to look into our own souls, we should immediately there discover that under the sun there neither exists nor *can* exist any work more thoroughly dignified—more supremely noble than this very poem—this poem *per se*—this poem which is a poem and nothing more—this poem written solely for the poem's sake.

With as deep a reverence for the True as ever inspired the bosom of man, I would, nevertheless, limit, in some measure, its modes of inculcation. I would limit to enforce them. I would not enfeeble them by dissipation. The demands of Truth are severe. She has no sympathy with the myrtles. All *that* which is so indispensable in Song, is precisely all *that* with which *she* has nothing whatever to do. It is but making her a flaunting paradox, to wreathe her in gems and flowers. In enforcing a truth, we need severity rather than efflorescence of language. We must be simple, precise, terse. We must be cool, calm, unimpassioned. In a word, we must be in that mood which, as nearly as possible, is the exact converse of the poetical. *He* must be blind indeed who does not perceive the radical and chasmal differences between the truthful and the poetical modes of inculcation. He must be theory-mad beyond redemption who, in spite of these differences, shall still persist in attempting to reconcile the obstinate oils and waters of Poetry and Truth.

Dividing the world of mind into its three most immediately obvious distinctions, we have the Pure Intellect, Taste, and the Moral Sense. I place Taste in the middle, because it is just this position which, in the mind, it occupies. It holds intimate relations with either extreme; but from the Moral Sense is separated by so faint a difference that Aristotle has not hesitated to place some of its operations among the virtues themselves. Nevertheless, we find the *offices* of the trio marked with a sufficient distinction. Just as the intellect concerns itself with Truth, so Taste informs us of the Beautiful, while the Moral Sense is regardful of Duty. Of this latter, while Conscience teaches the obligation, and Reason the expediency, Taste contents herself with displaying the charms:—waging war upon Vice solely on the ground of her deformity—her disproportion—her animosity to the fitting, to the appropriate, to the harmonious—in a word, to Beauty.

An immortal instinct, deep within the spirit of man, is thus, plainly, a sense of the Beautiful. This it is which administers to his delight in the manifold forms, and sounds, and odors, and sentiments amid which he exists. And just as the lily is repeated in the lake, or the eyes of Amaryllis in the mirror, so is the mere oral or written repetition of these forms, and sounds, and colors, and odors, and sentiments, a duplicate source of delight. But this mere repetition is not poetry. He who shall simply sing, with however glowing enthusiasm, or with however vivid a truth of description, of the sights, and sounds, and odors, and colors, and sentiments, which greet *him* in common with all mankind—he, I say, has yet failed to prove his divine title.

There is still a something in the distance which he has been unable to attain. We have still a thirst unquenchable, to allay which he has not shown us the crystal springs. This thirst belongs to the immortality of Man. It is at once a consequence and an indication of his perennial existence. It is the desire of the moth for the star. It is no mere appreciation of the Beauty before us—but a wild effort to reach the Beauty above. Inspired by an ecstatic prescience of the glories beyond the grave, we struggle, by multiform combinations among the things and thoughts of Time, to attain a portion of that Loveliness whose very elements, perhaps, appertain to eternity alone. And thus when by Poetry—or when by Music, the most entrancing of the Poetic moods —we find ourselves melted into tears—we weep then—not as the Abbaté Gravia supposes—through excess of pleasure, but through a certain petulant, impatient sorrow at our inability to grasp *now*, wholly, here on earth, at once and forever, those divine and rapturous joys, of which *through* the poem, or *through* the music, we attain to but brief and indeterminate glimpses.

The struggle to apprehend the supernal Loveliness—this struggle, on the part of souls fittingly constituted—has given to the world all *that* which it (the world) has ever been enabled at once to understand and *to feel* as poetic.

The Poetic Sentiment, of course, may develop itself in various modes—in Painting, in Sculpture, in Architecture, in the Dance— very especially in Music,—and very peculiarly, and with a wide field, in the composition of the Landscape Garden. Our present theme, however, has regard only to its manifestation in words. And here let me speak briefly on the topic of rhythm. Contenting myself with the certainty that Music, in its various modes of metre, rhythm, and rhyme, is of so vast a moment in Poetry as never to be wisely rejected—is so vitally important an adjunct, that he is simply silly who declines its assistance, I will not now pause to maintain its absolute essentiality. It is in Music, perhaps, that the soul most nearly attains the great end for which, when inspired by the Poetic Sentiment, it struggles—the creation of supernal Beauty. It *may* be, indeed, that here this sublime end is, now and then, attained *in fact*. We are often made to feel, with a shivering delight, that from an earthly harp are stricken notes which *cannot* have been unfamiliar to the angels. And thus there can be little doubt that in the union of Poetry with Music in its popular sense, we shall find the widest field for the Poetic development. The old Bards and Minnesingers had advantages which we do not possess—and Thomas Moore, singing his own songs, was, in the most legitimate manner, perfecting them as poems.

To recapitulate, then:—I would define, in brief, the Poetry of words as *The Rhythmical Creation of Beauty*. Its sole arbiter is Taste.

With the Intellect or with the Conscience, it has only collateral relations. Unless incidentally, it has no concern whatever either with Duty or with Truth.

A few words, however, in explanation. *That* pleasure which is at once the most pure, the most elevating, and the most intense, is derived, I maintain, from the contemplation of the Beautiful. In the contemplation of Beauty we alone find it possible to attain that pleasurable elevation, or excitement, *of the soul,* which we recognize as the Poetic Sentiment, and which is so easily distinguished from Truth, which is the satisfaction of the Reason, or from Passion, which is the excitement of the Heart. I make Beauty, therefore,—using the word as inclusive of the sublime,—I make Beauty the province of the poem, simply because it is an obvious rule of Art that effects should be made to spring as directly as possible from their causes:—no one as yet having been weak enough to deny that the peculiar elevation in question is at least *most readily* attainable in the poem. It by no means follows, however, that the incitements of Passion, or the precepts of Duty, or even the lessons of Truth, may not be introduced into a poem, and with advantage; for they may subserve, incidentally, in various ways, the general purposes of the work:—but the true artist will always contrive to tone them down in proper subjection to that *Beauty* which is the atmosphere and the real essence of the poem.

I cannot better introduce the few poems which I shall present for your consideration, than by the citation of the Proem to Mr. Longfellow's "Waif":

> The day is done, and the darkness
>   Falls from the wings of Night,
> As a feather is wafted downward
>   From an Eagle in his flight.
>
> I see the lights of the village
>   Gleam through the rain and the mist,
> And a feeling of sadness comes o'er me,
>   That my soul cannot resist;
>
> A feeling of sadness and longing,
>   That is not akin to pain,
> And resembles sorrow only
>   As the mist resembles the rain.
>
> Come, read to me some poem,
>   Some simple and heartfelt lay,
> That shall soothe this restless feeling,
>   And banish the thoughts of day.

85

Not from the grand old masters,
  Not from the bards sublime,
Whose distant footsteps echo
  Through the corridors of time.

For, like strains of martial music,
  Their mighty thoughts suggest
Life's endless toil and endeavor;
  And to-night I long for rest.

Read from some humbler poet,
  Whose songs gushed from his heart,
As showers from the clouds of summer,
  Or tears from the eyelids start;

Who through long days of labor,
  And nights devoid of ease,
Still heard in his soul the music
  Of wonderful melodies.

Such songs have power to quiet
  The restless pulse of care,
And come like the benediction
  That follows after prayer.

Then read from the treasured volume
  The poem of thy choice,
And lend to the rhyme of the poet
  The beauty of thy voice.

And the night shall be filled with music,
  And the cares, that infest the day,
Shall fold their tents, like the Arabs,
  And as silently steal away.

With no great range of imagination, these lines have been justly admired for their delicacy of expression. Some of the images are very effective. Nothing can be better than—

———————— the bards sublime,
Whose distant footsteps echo
  Through the corridors of time.

The idea of the last quatrain is also very effective. The poem, on the whole, however, is chiefly to be admired for the graceful *insouciance* of its metre, so well in accordance with the character of the sentiments, and especially for the *ease* of the general manner. This "ease," or naturalness, in a literary style, it has long been the fashion to regard as ease in appearance alone—as a point of really difficult attainment. But not so—a natural manner is difficult only to him who should never meddle with it—to the unnatural. It is but the result of writing with the understanding, or with the instinct, that *the tone,* in composition, should always be that which the mass of mankind would adopt —and must perpetually vary, of course, with the occasion. The author who, after the fashion of the *North American Review,* should be, upon *all* occasions, merely "quiet," must necessarily, upon *many* occasions, be simply silly, or stupid; and has no more right to be considered "easy," or "natural," than a Cockney exquisite, or than the sleeping Beauty in the wax-works.

Among the minor poems of Bryant, none has so much impressed me as the one which he entitles "June." I quote only a portion of it:

> There, through the long, long summer hours,
>   The golden light should lie,
> And thick, young herbs and groups of flowers
>   Stand in their beauty by.
> The oriole should build and tell
> The love-tale, close beside my cell;
>   The idle butterfly
> Should rest him there, and there be heard
> The housewife-bee and humming-bird.
>
> And what, if cheerful shouts, at noon,
>   Come, from the village sent,
> Or songs of maids, beneath the moon,
>   With fairy laughter blent?
> And what if, in the evening light,
> Betrothèd lovers walk in sight
>   Of my low monument?
> I would the lovely scene around
> Might know no sadder sight nor sound.
>
> I know that I no more should see
>   The season's glorious show,
> Nor would its brightness shine for me,
>   Nor its wild music flow;
> But if, around my place of sleep,
> The friends I love should come to weep,
>   They might not haste to go.
> Soft airs, and song, and light, and bloom
> Should keep them lingering by my tomb.

87

> These to their soften'd hearts should bear
>   The thought of what has been,
> And speak of one who cannot share
>   The gladness of the scene;
> Whose part in all the pomp that fills
> The circuit of the summer hills,
>   Is—that his grave is green;
> And deeply would their hearts rejoice
> To hear again his living voice.

The rhythmical flow, here, is even voluptuous—nothing could be more melodious. The poem has always affected me in a remarkable manner. The intense melancholy which seems to well up, perforce, to the surface of all the poet's cheerful sayings about his grave, we find thrilling us to the soul—while there is the truest poetic elevation in the thrill. The impression left is one of a pleasurable sadness. And if, in the remaining compositions which I shall introduce to you, there be more or less of a similar tone always apparent, let me remind you that (how or why we know not) this certain taint of sadness is inseparably connected with all the higher manifestations of true Beauty. It is, nevertheless,

> A feeling of sadness and longing,
>   That is not akin to pain,
> And resembles sorrow only
>   As the mist resembles the rain.

The taint of which I speak is clearly perceptible even in a poem so full of brilliancy and spirit as the "Health" of Edward C. Pinkney:

> I fill this cup to one made up
>   Of loveliness alone,
> A woman, of her gentle sex
>   The seeming paragon;
> To whom the better elements
>   And kindly stars have given
> A form so fair, that, like the air,
>   'T is less of earth than heaven.
>
> Her every tone is music's own,
>   Like those of morning birds,
> And something more than melody
>   Dwells ever in her words:
> The coinage of her heart are they,
>   And from her lips each flows
> As one may see the burden'd bee
>   Forth issue from the rose.

Affections are as thoughts to her,
    The measures of her hours;
Her feelings have the fragrancy,
    The freshness of young flowers;
And lovely passions, changing oft,
    So fill her, she appears
The image of themselves by turns,—
    The idol of past years!

Of her bright face one glance will trace
    A picture on the brain,
And of her voice in echoing hearts
    A sound must long remain;
But memory, such as mine of her,
    So very much endears,
When death is nigh my latest sigh
    Will not be life's, but hers.

I fill this cup to one made up
    Of loveliness alone,
A woman, of her gentle sex
    The seeming paragon—
Her health! and would on earth there stood
    Some more of such a frame,
That life might be all poetry,
    And weariness a name.

It was the misfortune of Mr. Pinkney to have been born too far south. Had he been a New Englander, it is probable that he would have been ranked as the first of American lyrists, by that magnanimous cabal which has so long controlled the destinies of American Letters, in conducting the thing called the *North American Review*. The poem just cited is especially beautiful; but the poetic elevation which it induces, we must refer chiefly to our sympathy in the poet's enthusiasm. We pardon his hyperboles for the evident earnestness with which they are uttered.

It is by no means my design, however, to expatiate upon the *merits* of what I should read you. These will necessarily speak for themselves. Boccalini, in his "Advertisements from Parnassus," tells us that Zoilus once presented Apollo a very caustic criticism upon a very admirable book—whereupon the god asked him for the beauties of the work. He replied that he only busied himself about the errors. On hearing this, Apollo, handing him a sack of unwinnowed wheat, bade him pick out *all the chaff* for his reward.

Now that fable answers very well as a hit at the critics—but I am by no means sure that the god was in the right. I am by no means certain that the true limits of the critical duty are not grossly misunderstood. Excellence, in a poem especially, may be considered in the light of an axiom, which need only be properly *put* to become self-evident. It is *not* excellence if it requires to be demonstrated as such: —and thus, to point out too particularly the merits of a work of Art, is to admit that they are *not* merits altogether.

Among the "Melodies" of Thomas Moore, is one whose distinguished character as a poem proper seems to have been singularly left out of view. I allude to his lines beginning: "Come, rest in this bosom." The intense energy of their expression is not surpassed by anything in Byron. There are two of the lines in which a sentiment is conveyed that embodies the *all in all* of the divine passion of Love—a sentiment which, perhaps, has found its echo in more, and in more passionate, human hearts than any other single sentiment ever embodied in words:

> Come, rest in this bosom, my own stricken deer,
> Though the herd have fled from thee, thy home is still here;
> Here still is the smile that no cloud can o'ercast,
> And a heart and a hand all thy own to the last.
>
> Oh! what was love made for, if 't is not the same
> Through joy and through torment, through glory and shame?
> I know not, I ask not, if guilt 's in that heart,
> I but know that I love thee, whatever thou art.
>
> Thou hast call'd me thy Angel in moments of bliss,
> And thy Angel I 'll be, 'mid the horrors of this,—
> Through the furnace, unshrinking, thy steps to pursue,
> And shield thee, and save thee,—or perish there too!

It has been the fashion, of late days, to deny Moore Imagination, while granting him Fancy—a distinction originating with Coleridge —than whom no man more fully comprehended the great powers of Moore. The fact is, that the fancy of this poet so far predominates over all his other faculties, and over the fancy of all other men, as to have induced, very naturally, the idea that he is fanciful *only*. But never was there a greater mistake. Never was a grosser wrong done the fame of a true poet. In the compass of the English language I can call to mind no poem more profoundly, more weirdly *imaginative*, in the best sense, than the lines commencing: "I would I were by that dim lake," which are the composition of Thomas Moore. I regret that I am unable to remember them.

One of the noblest—and, speaking of Fancy, one of the most singularly fanciful—of modern poets, was Thomas Hood. His "Fair Ines" had always, for me, an inexpressible charm:—

> Oh! saw ye not fair Ines?
>   She's gone into the West,
> To dazzle when the sun is down,
>   And rob the world of rest:
> She took our daylight with her,
>   The smiles that we love best,
> With morning blushes on her cheek,
>   And pearls upon her breast.
>
> Oh! turn again, fair Ines,
>   Before the fall of night,
> For fear the moon should shine alone,
>   And stars unrivall'd bright;
> And blessèd will the lover be
>   That walks beneath their light,
> And breathes the love against thy cheek
>   I dare not even write!
>
> Would I had been, fair Ines,
>   That gallant cavalier,
> Who rode so gaily by thy side,
>   And whisper'd thee so near!
> Were there no bonny dames at home,
>   Or no true lovers here,
> That he should cross the seas to win
>   The dearest of the dear?
>
> I saw thee, lovely Ines,
>   Descend along the shore,
> With bands of noble gentlemen,
>   And banners waved before;
> And gentle youth and maidens gay,
>   And snowy plumes they wore;
> It would have been a beauteous dream,
>   —If it had been no more!
>
> Alas, alas, fair Ines!
>   She went away with song,
> With Music waiting on her steps,
>   And shoutings of the throng;
> But some were sad and felt no mirth,

But only Music's wrong,
In sounds that sang Farewell, Farewell,
To her you 've loved so long.

Farewell, farewell, fair Ines,
That vessel never bore
So fair a lady on its deck,
Nor danced so light before.
Alas for pleasure on the sea,
And sorrow on the shore!
The smile that blessed one lover's heart
Has broken many more.

"The Haunted House," by the same author, is one of the truest poems ever written—one of the *truest*—one of the most unexceptionable—one of the most thoroughly artistic, both in its theme and in its execution. It is, moreover, powerfully ideal—imaginative. I regret that its length renders it unsuitable for the purposes of this Lecture. In place of it, permit me to offer the universally appreciated "Bridge of Sighs."

One more unfortunate,
Weary of breath,
Rashly importunate,
Gone to her death!

Take her up tenderly,
Lift her with care;
Fashion'd so slenderly,
Young, and so fair!

Look at her garments
Clinging like cerements;
Whilst the wave constantly
Drips from her clothing;
Take her up instantly,
Loving, not loathing.—

Touch her not scornfully;
Think of her mournfully,
Gently and humanly;
Not of the stains of her,
All that remains of her
Now, is pure womanly.

Make no deep scrutiny
Into her mutiny
Rash and undutiful:
Past all dishonor,
Death has left on her
Only the beautiful.

Still, for all slips of hers,
One of Eve's family—
Wipe those poor lips of hers
Oozing so clammily.

Loop up her tresses
Escaped from the comb,
Her fair auburn tresses;
Whilst wonderment guesses
Where was her home?

Who was her father?
Who was her mother?
Had she a sister?
Had she a brother?
Or was there a dearer one
Still, and a nearer one
Yet, than all other?

Alas! for the rarity
Of Christian charity
Under the sun!
Oh, it was pitiful!
Near a whole city full,
Home she had none.

Sisterly, brotherly,
Fatherly, motherly
Feelings had changed:
Love, by harsh evidence
Thrown from its eminence;
Even God's providence
Seeming estranged.

Where the lamps quiver
So far in the river,
With many a light

From window and casement,
From garret to basement,
She stood, with amazement,
Houseless by night.

The bleak wind of March
Made her tremble and shiver;
But not the dark arch,
Or the black flowing river:
Mad from life's history,
Glad to death's mystery,
Swift to be hurl'd—
Anywhere, anywhere
Out of the world!

In she plunged boldly,
No matter how coldly
The rough river ran,—
Over the brink of it,
Picture it—think of it,
Dissolute man!
Lave in it, drink of it
Then, if you can!

Take her up tenderly,
Lift her with care;
Fashion'd so slenderly,
Young, and so fair!

Ere her limbs frigidly
Stiffen too rigidly,
Decently,—kindly,—
Smooth, and compose them
And her eyes, close them,
Staring so blindly!

Dreadfully staring
Through muddy impurity,
As when with the daring
Last look of despairing
Fixed on futurity.

Perishing gloomily,
Spurred by contumely,

Cold inhumanity,
Burning insanity,
Into her rest.—
Cross her hands humbly,
As if praying dumbly,
Over her breast!

Owning her weakness,
Her evil behavior,
And leaving, with meekness,
Her sins to her Savior!

The vigor of this poem is no less remarkable than its pathos. The versification, although carrying the fanciful to the very verge of the fantastic, is nevertheless admirably adapted to the wild insanity which is the thesis of the poem.

Among the minor poems of Lord Byron, is one which has never received from the critics the praise which it undoubtedly deserves:

Though the day of my destiny's over,
    And the star of my fate hath declined,
Thy soft heart refused to discover
    The faults which so many could find;
Though thy soul with my grief was acquainted
    It shrunk not to share it with me,
And the love which my spirit hath painted
    It never hath found but in *thee*.

Then when nature around me is smiling,
    The last smile which answers to mine,
I do not believe it beguiling,
    Because it reminds me of thine;
And when winds are at war with the ocean,
    As the breasts I believed in with me,
If their billows excite an emotion,
    It is that they bear me from *thee*.

Though the rock of my last hope shivered,
    And its fragments are sunk in the wave,
Though I feel that my soul is delivered
    To pain—it shall not be its slave.
There is many a pang to pursue me;
    They may crush, but they shall not contemn;
They may torture, but shall not subdue me;
    'T is of *thee* that I think—not of them.

95

Though human, thou didst not deceive me;
    Though woman, thou didst not forsake;
Though loved, thou foreborest to grieve me;
    Though slandered, thou never couldst shake;
Though trusted, thou didst not disclaim me;
    Though parted, it was not to fly;
Though watchful, 't was not to defame me
    Nor mute, that the world might belie.

Yet I blame not the world, nor despise it,
    Nor the war of the many with one—
If my soul was not fitted to prize it,
    'T was folly not sooner to shun:
And if dearly that error hath cost me,
    And more than I once could foresee,
I have found that whatever it lost me,
    It could not deprive me of *thee*.

From the wreck of the past, which hath perished,
    Thus much I at least may recall:
It hath taught me that which I most cherished
    Deserved to be dearest of all.
In the desert a fountain is springing,
    In the wide waste there still is a tree,
And a bird in the solitude singing,
    Which speaks to my spirit of *thee*.

Although the rhythm, here, is one of the most difficult, the versification could scarcely be improved. No nobler *theme* ever engaged the pen of poet. It is the soul-elevating idea, that no man can consider himself entitled to complain of Fate while, in his adversity, he still retains the unwavering love of woman.

From Alfred Tennyson—although in perfect sincerity I regard him as the noblest poet that ever lived—I have left myself time to cite only a very brief specimen. I call him, and *think* him the noblest of poets—*not* because the impressions he produces are, at *all* times, the most profound—*not* because the poetical excitement which he induces is, at *all* times, the most intense—but because it *is*, at all times, the most ethereal—in other words, the most elevating and the most pure. No poet is so little of the earth, earthy. What I am about to read is from his last long poem, "The Princess":

Tears, idle tears, I know not what they mean,
Tears from the depth of some divine despair
Rise in the heart, and gather to the eyes,

In looking on the happy autumn-fields,
And thinking of the days that are no more.

Fresh as the first beam glittering on a sail
That brings our friends up from the underworld,
Sad as the last which reddens over me
That sinks with all we love below the verge;
So sad, so fresh, the days that are no more.

Ah, sad and strange as in dark summer dawns
The earliest pipe of half-awaken'd birds
To dying ears, when unto dying eyes
The casement slowly grows a glimmering square;
So sad, so strange, the days that are no more.

Dear as remember'd kisses after death,
And sweet as those by hopeless fancy feign'd
On lips that are for others; deep as love,
Deep as first love, and wild with all regret;
O Death in Life, the days that are no more!

Thus, although in a very cursory and imperfect manner, I have endeavored to convey to you my conception of the Poetic Principle. It has been my purpose to suggest that, while this Principle itself is, strictly and simply, the Human Aspiration for Supernal Beauty, the manifestation of the Principle is always found in *an elevating excitement of the Soul*—quite independent of that passion which is the intoxication of the Heart—or of that Truth which is the satisfaction of the Reason. For, in regard to Passion, alas! its tendency is to degrade, rather than to elevate the Soul. Love, on the contrary—Love—the true, the divine Eros—the Uranian, as distinguished from the Dionæan Venus—is unquestionably the purest and truest of all poetical themes. And in regard to Truth—if, to be sure, through the attainment of truth, we are led to perceive a harmony where none was apparent before, we experience, at once, the true poetical effect—but this effect is referable to the harmony alone, and not in the least degree to the truth which merely served to render the harmony manifest.

We shall reach, however, more immediately a distinct conception of what the true Poetry is, by mere reference to a few of the simple elements which induce in the Poet himself the true poetical effect. He recognizes the ambrosia which nourishes his soul, in the bright orbs that shine in Heaven—in the volutes of the flower—in the clustering of low shrubberies—in the waving of the grain-fields—in the slanting of tall, Eastern trees—in the blue distance of mountains—in the grouping of clouds—in the twinkling of half-hidden brooks—in the gleaming of silver rivers—in the repose of sequestered lakes—in the star-mirroring depths of lonely wells. He perceives it in the songs of birds—in the harp of Æolus—in the sighing of the night-wind—in the repining voice of the forest—in the surf that complains to the shore—in the fresh breath of the woods—in the scent of the violet—in the voluptuous perfume of the hyacinth—in the suggestive odor that comes to him, at eventide, from far-distant, undiscovered islands, over dim oceans, illimitable and unexplored. He owns it in all noble thoughts—in all unworldly motives—in all holy impulses—in all chivalrous, generous, and self-sacrificing deeds. He feels it in the beauty of woman—in the grace of her step—in the lustre of her eye —in the melody of her voice—in her soft laughter—in her sigh—in the harmony of the rustling of her robes. He deeply feels it in her winning endearments—in her burning enthusiasms—in her gentle charities—in her meek and devotional endurances—but above all— ah, far above all—he kneels to it—he worships it in the faith, in the purity, in the strength, in the altogether divine majesty—of her *love*.

Let me conclude by the recitation of yet another brief poem—one very different in character from any that I have before quoted. It is by Motherwell, and is called "The Song of the Cavalier." With our modern and altogether rational ideas of the absurdity and impiety of warfare, we are not precisely in that frame of mind best adapted to sympathize with the sentiments, and thus to appreciate the real excellence, of the poem. To do this fully, we must identify ourselves, in fancy, with the soul of the old cavalier.

> Then mounte! then mounte, brave gallants, all,
>   And don your helmes amaine:
> Deathe's couriers, Fame and Honour, call
>   Us to the field againe.
>
> No shrewish teares shall fill our eye
>   When the sword-hilt 's in our hand;
> Heart-whole we'll part and no whit sighe
>   For the fayrest of the land;
> Let piping swaine, and craven wight,
>   Thus weepe and puling crye,
> Our business is like men to fight,
>   And hero-like to die!

The Poems of Edgar Allan Poe

VI

POEMS ADDED IN THE EDITION OF 1845

The Editor's Commentary

THE RAVEN AND OTHER POEMS was published at the end of 1845, when Poe was thirty-six. It comprised thirty poems in all—the carefully pruned work of two decades and a dozen other poems that had appeared in various magazines. Some of the new poems were already popular, for Poe had recited them on public platforms and at private soirées. "The Raven" had become the favorite poem of the period. It was quoted everywhere; when an actor interpolated "Nevermore, nevermore" into his lines "a thrill ran through the audience and a profound sensation was produced."

Today "The Raven," with its semi-comic internal rhymes and its obvious theatricality, seems a relic of the elocutionist's repertoire. It almost justifies Emerson's characterization of Poe as "the jingle man," and makes Poe's own account of its origins in "The Philosophy of Composition" (see page 205), seem suspiciously like reasoning after the event. Poe ridiculed the assumption that "The Raven" was the result of "a fine frenzy" or that it was suggested by any other source except a carefully planned program of "effects." Yet Poe had admired the basic structure long before he claimed it as his own. He had found it in Elizabeth Barrett Browning's poem "Lady Geraldine's Courtship," and Poe's:

"And the silken sad uncertain rustling of each purple curtain"

was more than a mere approximation—rhythm, rhyme-scheme, and the very color—of Mrs. Browning's:

"With a murmurous stir uncertain in the air the purple curtain—."

Perhaps in tribute, perhaps in compensation, Poe dedicated *The Raven and Other Poems* to "the Noblest of her Sex, the author of 'The Drama in Exile'—to Miss Elizabeth Barrett of England."

The lyrics "To F—" and "To F—s S. O—d" were inscribed to Frances Sargent Osgood, author of "Call me pet names, dearest! Call me a bird!" but, in spite of their devoted tone, they had previously been dedicated to other ladies. "To One in Paradise," with its magic beginning and ending, is sometimes thought to be an elegy to Poe's child-wife; but the poem, originally entitled "The Visionary," was first published in 1835, twelve years before Virginia's death.

The Raven

Once upon a midnight dreary, while I pondered, weak and weary,
Over many a quaint and curious volume of forgotten lore,
　While I nodded, nearly napping, suddenly there came a tapping,
　As of some one gently rapping, rapping at my chamber door.
" 'Tis some visitor," I muttered, "tapping at my chamber door—
　　　　Only this, and nothing more."

Ah, distinctly I remember it was in the bleak December,
And each separate dying ember wrought its ghost upon the floor.
　Eagerly I wished the morrow;—vainly I had sought to borrow
　From my books surcease of sorrow—sorrow for the lost Lenore—
For the rare and radiant maiden whom the angels name Lenore—
　　　　Nameless here for evermore.

And the silken sad uncertain rustling of each purple curtain
Thrilled me—filled me with fantastic terrors never felt before;
　So that now, to still the beating of my heart, I stood repeating,
　" 'Tis some visitor entreating entrance at my chamber door—
Some late visitor entreating entrance at my chamber door;—
　　　　This it is, and nothing more."

Presently my soul grew stronger; hesitating then no longer,
"Sir," said I, "or Madam, truly your forgiveness I implore;
　But the fact is I was napping, and so gently you came rapping,
　And so faintly you came tapping, tapping at my chamber door,
That I scarce was sure I heard you"—here I opened wide the door;—
　　　　Darkness there, and nothing more.

Deep into that darkness peering, long I stood there wondering,
　　　fearing,
Doubting, dreaming dreams no mortals ever dared to dream before;
　But the silence was unbroken, and the stillness gave no token,
　And the only word there spoken was the whispered word, "Lenore!"
This I whispered, and an echo murmured back the word, "Lenore!"—
　　　　Merely this, and nothing more.

Back into the chamber turning, all my soul within me burning,
Soon again I heard a tapping somewhat louder than before.
　"Surely," said I, "surely that is something at my window lattice:
　Let me see, then, what thereat is, and this mystery explore—
Let my heart be still a moment and this mystery explore;—
　　　　'Tis the wind and nothing more."

Open here I flung the shutter, when, with many a flirt and flutter,
In there stepped a stately raven of the saintly days of yore;
    Not the least obeisance made he; not a minute stopped or stayed he;
    But, with mien of lord or lady, perched above my chamber door—
Perched upon a bust of Pallas just above my chamber door—
        Perched, and sat, and nothing more.

Then this ebony bird beguiling my sad fancy into smiling,
By the grave and stern decorum of the countenance it wore.
    "Though thy crest be shorn and shaven, thou," I said, "art sure no craven,
    Ghastly grim and ancient raven wandering from the Nightly shore—
Tell me what thy lordly name is on the Night's Plutonian shore!"
        Quoth the Raven, "Nevermore."

Much I marvelled this ungainly fowl to hear discourse so plainly,
Though its answer little meaning—little relevancy bore;
    For we cannot help agreeing that no living human being
    Ever yet was blest with seeing bird above his chamber door—
Bird or beast upon the sculptured bust above his chamber door,
        With such name as "Nevermore."

But the raven, sitting lonely on the placid bust, spoke only
That one word, as if his soul in that one word he did outpour.
    Nothing further then he uttered—not a feather then he fluttered—
    Till I scarcely more than muttered, "other friends have flown before—
On the morrow *he* will leave me, as my hopes have flown before."
        Then the bird said, "Nevermore."

Startled at the stillness broken by reply so aptly spoken,
"Doubtless," said I, "what it utters is its only stock and store,
    Caught from some unhappy master whom unmerciful Disaster
    Followed fast and followed faster till his songs one burden bore—
Till the dirges of his Hope that melancholy burden bore
        Of 'Never—nevermore'."

But the Raven still beguiling all my fancy into smiling,
Straight I wheeled a cushioned seat in front of bird, and bust and door;
    Then upon the velvet sinking, I betook myself to linking
    Fancy unto fancy, thinking what this ominous bird of yore—
What this grim, ungainly, ghastly, gaunt and ominous bird of yore
        Meant in croaking "Nevermore."

THE RAVEN

This I sat engaged in guessing, but no syllable expressing
To the fowl whose fiery eyes now burned into my bosom's core;
   This and more I sat divining, with my head at ease reclining
   On the cushion's velvet lining that the lamplight gloated o'er,
But whose velvet violet lining with the lamplight gloating o'er,
          She shall press, ah, nevermore!

Then methought the air grew denser, perfumed from an unseen
       censer
Swung by Seraphim whose footfalls tinkled on the tufted floor.
   "Wretch," I cried, "thy God hath lent thee—by these angels he
       hath sent thee
Respite—respite and nepenthe, from thy memories of Lenore!
Quaff, oh quaff this kind nepenthe and forget this lost Lenore!"
          Quoth the Raven, "Nevermore."

"Prophet!" said I, "thing of evil!—prophet still, if bird or devil!—
Whether Tempter sent, or whether tempest tossed thee here ashore,
   Desolate yet all undaunted, on this desert land enchanted—
   On this home by horror haunted—tell me truly, I implore—
Is there—*is* there balm in Gilead?—tell me—tell me, I implore!"
          Quoth the Raven, "Nevermore."

"Prophet!" said I, "thing of evil—prophet still, if bird or devil!
By that Heaven that bends above us—by that God we both adore—
   Tell this soul with sorrow laden if, within the distant Aidenn,
   It shall clasp a sainted maiden whom the angels name Lenore—
Clasp a rare and radiant maiden whom the angels name Lenore."
          Quoth the Raven, "Nevermore."

"Be that word our sign in parting, bird or fiend," I shrieked, upstarting—
"Get thee back into the tempest and the Night's Plutonian shore!
   Leave no black plume as a token of that lie thy soul hath spoken!
   Leave my loneliness unbroken!—quit the bust above my door!
Take thy beak from out my heart, and take thy form from off my door!"
          Quoth the Raven, "Nevermore."

And the Raven, never flitting, still is sitting, still is sitting
On the pallid bust of Pallas just above my chamber door;
   And his eyes have all the seeming of a demon's that is dreaming,
   And the lamplight o'er him streaming throws his shadow on the
       floor;
And my soul from out that shadow that lies floating on the floor
          Shall be lifted—nevermore!

105

The Haunted Palace

In the greenest of our valleys
   By good angels tenanted,
Once a fair and stately palace—
   Radiant palace—reared its head.
In the monarch Thought's dominion—
   It stood there!
Never seraph spread a pinion
   Over fabric half so fair!

Banners yellow, glorious, golden,
   On its roof did float and flow,
(This—all this—was in the olden
   Time long ago,)
And every gentle air that dallied,
   In that sweet day,
Along the ramparts plumed and pallid,
   A wingèd odor went away.

Wanderers in that happy valley,
   Through two luminous windows, saw
Spirits moving musically,
   To a lute's well-tunèd law,
Round about a throne where, sitting
   (Porphyrogene!)
In state his glory well-befitting,
   The ruler of the realm was seen.

And all with pearl and ruby glowing
   Was the fair palace door,
Through which came flowing, flowing, flowing,
   And sparkling evermore,
A troop of Echoes, whose sweet duty
   Was but to sing,
In voices of surpassing beauty,
   The wit and wisdom of their king.

But evil things, in robes of sorrow,
   Assailed the monarch's high estate.
(Ah, let us mourn!—for never morrow
   Shall dawn upon him desolate!)
And round about his home the glory
   That blushed and bloomed,
Is but a dim-remembered story
   Of the old time entombed.

And travellers, now, within that valley,
　　Through the red-litten windows see
Vast forms, that move fantastically
　　To a discordant melody,
While, like a ghastly rapid river,
　　Through the pale door
A hideous throng rush out forever
　　And laugh—but smile no more.

To One in Paradise

Thou wast all that to me, love,
　　For which my soul did pine—
A green isle in the sea, love,
　　A fountain and a shrine,
All wreathed with fairy fruits and flowers,
　　And all the flowers were mine.

Ah, dream too bright to last!
　　Ah, starry Hope! that didst arise
But to be overcast!
　　A voice from out the Future cries,
"On! on!"—but o'er the Past
　　(Dim gulf!) my spirit hovering lies
Mute, motionless, aghast!

For, alas! alas! with me
　　The light of Life is o'er!
　　"No more—no more—no more—"
(Such language holds the solemn sea
　　To the sands upon the shore)
Shall bloom the thunder-blasted tree
　　Or the stricken eagle soar!

And all my days are trances,
　　And all my nightly dreams
Are where thy grey eye glances,
　　And where thy footstep gleams—
In what ethereal dances,
　　By what eternal streams.

Bridal Ballad

The ring is on my hand,
　And the wreath is on my brow;
Satin and jewels grand
Are all at my command,
　And I am happy now.

And my lord he loves me well;
　But, when first he breathed his vow,
I felt my bosom swell—
For the words rang as a knell,
And the voice seemed *his* who fell
In the battle down the dell,
　And who is happy now.

But he spoke to re-assure me,
　And he kissed my pallid brow,
While a reverie came o'er me,
And to the church-yard bore me,
And I sighed to him before me,
Thinking him dead D'Elormie,
　"Oh, I am happy now!"

And thus the words were spoken,
　And this the plighted vow,
And, though my faith be broken,
And, though my heart be broken,
Here is a ring, as token
　That I am happy now!

Would God I could awaken!
　For I dream I know not how!
And my soul is sorely shaken
Lest an evil step be taken,—
Lest the dead who is forsaken
　May not be happy now.

Scenes from "Politian"

DRAMATIS PERSONAE

POLITIAN, Earl of Leicester.
DI BROGLIO, a Roman Duke.
COUNT CASTIGLIONE, his son.
BALDAZZAR, Duke of Surrey,
    Friend to Politian.

A MONK.
LALAGE
ALESSANDRA, betrothed to Casti-
    glione.
JACINTA, maid to Lalage.

The Scene lies in Rome

I

ROME—*A Hall in a Palace*

ALESSANDRA *and* CASTIGLIONE

ALESSANDRA

Thou art sad, Castiglione.

CASTIGLIONE
            Sad!—not I.
Oh, I'm the happiest, happiest man in Rome!
A few days more, thou knowest, my Alessandra,
Will make thee mine. Oh, I am very happy!

ALESSANDRA

Methinks thou hast a singular way of showing
Thy happiness!—what ails thee, cousin of mine?
Why didst thou sigh so deeply?

CASTIGLIONE
            Did I sigh?
I was not conscious of it. It is a fashion,
A silly—a most silly fashion I have
When I am *very* happy. Did I sigh?   *(Sighing)*

ALESSANDRA

Thou didst. Thou art not well. Thou hast indulged
Too much of late, and I am vexed to see it.
Late hours and wine, Castiglione,—these
Will ruin thee! thou art already altered—
Thy looks are haggard—nothing so wears away
The constitution as late hours and wine.

CASTIGLIONE (*musing*)

Nothing, fair cousin, nothing—not even deep sorrow—
Wears it away like evil hours and wine.
I will amend.

ALESSANDRA

Do it! I would have thee drop
Thy riotous company, too—fellows low born—
Ill suit the like with old Di Broglio's heir
And Alessandra's husband.

CASTIGLIONE

I will drop them.

ALESSANDRA

Thou wilt—thou must. Attend thou also more
To thy dress and equippage—they are over plain
For thy lofty rank and fashion—much depends
Upon appearances.

CASTIGLIONE

I'll see to it.

ALESSANDRA

Then see to it!—pay more attention, sir,
To a becoming carriage—much thou wantest
In dignity.

CASTIGLIONE

Much, much, oh! much I want
In proper dignity.

ALESSANDRA (*haughtily*)

Thou mockest me, sir.

CASTIGLIONE (*abstractedly*)

Sweet, gentle Lalage!

ALESSANDRA

Heard I aright?
speak to him—he speaks of Lalage!
Sir Count! (*places her hand on his shoulder*) what art thou dreaming?
(*aside*) He's not well!
What ails thee, sir?

110

CASTIGLIONE (*starting*)
Cousin! fair cousin!—madam!
I crave thy pardon—indeed I am not well—
Your hand from off my shoulder, if you please.
This air is most oppressive!—Madam—the Duke!
(*Enter* DI BROGLIO)

DI BROGLIO
My son, I've news for thee!—hey?—what's the matter? (*observing
Alessandra*)
I' the pouts? Kiss her, Castiglione! kiss her,
You dog! and make it up, I say, this minute!
I've news for you both. Politian is expected
Hourly in Rome—Politian, Earl of Leicester!
We'll have him at the wedding. 'Tis his first visit
To the imperial city.

ALESSANDRA
What! Politian
Of Britain, Earl of Leicester?

DI BROGLIO
The same, my love.
We'll have him at the wedding. A man quite young
In years, but grey in fame. I have not seen him,
But Rumour speaks of him as of a prodigy
Preëminent in arts and arms, and wealth,
And high descent. We'll have him at the wedding.

ALESSANDRA
I have heard much of this Politian.
Gay, volatile and giddy—is he not?
And little given to thinking.

DI BROGLIO
Far from it, love.
No branch, they say, of all philosophy
So deep abstruse he has not mastered it.
Learned as few are learned.

ALESSANDRA
'Tis very strange!
I have known men have seen Politian
And sought his company. They speak of him

111

As of one who entered madly into life,
Drinking the cup of pleasure to the dregs.

CASTIGLIONE

Ridiculous! Now *I* have seen Politian
And know him well—nor learned nor mirthful he.
He is a dreamer, and a man shut out
From common passions.

DI BROGLIO
                    Children, we disagree.
Let us go forth and taste the fragrant air
Of the garden. Did I dream, or did I hear
Politian was a *melancholy* man?   *(Exeunt)*

II

ROME—*A Lady's apartment, with a window open and looking into a
    garden.* LALAGE, *in deep mourning, reading at a table on which lie
    some books and a hand mirror. In the background* JACINTA *(a ser-
    vant maid) leans carelessly upon a chair.*

LALAGE

Jacinta, is it thou?

JACINTA *(pertly)*
Yes, ma'am, I'm here.

LALAGE

I did not know, Jacinta, you were in waiting.
Sit down!—let not my presence trouble you—
Sit down!—for I am humble, most humble.

JACINTA *(aside)*
                    'Tis time.
(JACINTA *seats herself in a side-long manner upon the chair,
    resting her elbows upon the back, and regarding her mis-
    tress with a contemptuous look.* LALAGE *continues to read.*)

LALAGE

"It in another climate, so he said,
"Bore a bright golden flower, but not i' this soil!"
                    (pauses—turns over some leaves, and resumes)

112

"No lingering winters there, nor snow, nor shower—
"But Ocean ever to refresh mankind
"Breathes the shrill spirit of the western wind."
O, beautiful!—most beautiful!—how like
To what my fevered soul doth dream of Heaven!
O happy land! *(pauses)* She died!—the maiden died!
A still more happy maiden who couldst die!
Jacinta!

      (JACINTA *returns no answer, and* LALAGE *presently resumes*)
Again!—a similar tale
Told of a beauteous dame beyond the sea!
Thus speaketh one Ferdinand in the words of the play—
"She died full young"—one Bossola answers him—
"I think not so—her infelicity
"Seemed to have years too many"—Ah luckless lady!
Jacinta! *(still no answer)*
              Here 's a far sterner story,
But like—oh, very like in its despair—
Of that Egyptian queen, winning so easily
A thousand hearts—losing at length her own.
She died. Thus endeth the history—and her maids
Lean over and weep—two gentle maids
With gentle names—Eiros and Charmion!
Rainbow and Dove!——Jacinta!

            JACINTA *(pettishly)*
             Madam, what *is* it?

            LALAGE
Wilt thou, my good Jacinta, be so kind
As go down in the library and bring me
The Holy Evangelists?
            JACINTA
         Pshaw!   *(Exit)*

            LALAGE
          If there be balm
For the wounded spirit in Gilead it is there!
Dew in the night-time of my bitter trouble
Will there be found—"dew sweeter far than that
Which hangs like chains of pearl on Hermon hill."

        (Re-enter JACINTA, *and throws a volume on the table*)
There, ma'am, 's the book. Indeed she is very troublesome.   *(Aside)*

113

LALAGE *(astonished)*
What didst thou say, Jacinta? Have I done aught
To grieve thee or to vex thee?—I am sorry.
For thou hast served me long and ever been
Trustworthy and respectful.   *(resumes her reading)*

JACINTA *(aside)*
I can't believe
She has any more jewels—no—no—she gave me all.

LALAGE
What didst thou say, Jacinta? Now I bethink me
Thou hast not spoken lately of thy wedding.
How fares good Ugo?—and when is it to be?
Can I do aught?—is there no farther aid
Thou needest, Jacinta?

JACINTA
Is there no *farther* aid!
That's meant for me *(aside)*. I'm sure, madam, you need not
Be always throwing those jewels in my teeth.

LALAGE
Jewels! Jacinta,—now indeed, Jacinta,
I thought not of the jewels.

JACINTA
Oh! perhaps not!
But then I might have sworn it. After all,
There 's Ugo says the ring is only paste,
For he 's sure the Count Castiglione never
Would have given a real diamond to such as you;
And at the best I'm certain, madam, you cannot
Have use for jewels *now*. But I might have sworn it.   *(Exit)*
         (LALAGE *bursts into tears and leans her head upon the table
         —after a short pause raises it)*

LALAGE
Poor Lalage!—and is it come to this?
Thy servant maid!—but courage!—'tis but a viper
Whom thou hast cherished to sting thee to the soul!
                         (Taking up the mirror)
Ha! here at least 's a friend—too much a friend
In earlier days—a friend will not deceive thee.

114

Fair mirror and true! now tell me (for thou canst)
A tale—a pretty tale—and heed thou not
Though it be rife with woe. It answers me.
It speaks of sunken eyes, and wasted cheeks,
And Beauty long deceased—remembers me
Of Joy departed—Hope, the Seraph Hope,
Inurnèd and entombed:—now, in a tone
Low, sad, and solemn, but most audible,
Whispers of early grave untimely yawning
For ruined maid. Fair mirror and true—thou liest not!
Thou hast no end to gain—no heart to break—
Castiglione lied who said he loved—
Thou true—he false!—false!—false!

> (*While she speaks, a monk enters her apartment, and approaches unobserved*)

MONK

                    Refuge thou hast,
Sweet daughter, in Heaven. Think of eternal things!
Give up thy soul to penitence, and pray!

LALAGE (*arising hurriedly*)

I *cannot* pray!—My soul is at war with God!
The frightful sounds of merriment below
Disturb my senses—go! I cannot pray—
The sweet airs from the garden worry me!
Thy presence grieves me—go!—thy priestly raiment
Fills me with dread—thy ebony crucifix
With horror and awe!

MONK

Think of thy precious soul!

LALAGE

Think of my early days!—think of my father
And mother in Heaven! think of our quiet home,
And the rivulet that ran before the door!
Think of my little sisters!—think of them!
And think of me!—think of my trusting love
And confidence—his vows—my ruin—think—think
Of my unspeakable misery!—begone!
Yet stay! yet stay!—what was it thou saidst of prayer
And penitence? Didst thou not speak of faith
And vows before the throne?

115

MONK
I did.

LALAGE
                                        'Tis well.
There *is* a vow were fitting should be made—
A sacred vow, imperative, and urgent,
A solemn vow!

MONK
Daughter, this zeal is well.

LALAGE
Father, this zeal is anything but well!
Hast thou a crucifix fit for this thing?
A crucifix whereon to register
This sacred vow?   *(He hands her his own)*
Not that—Oh! no!—no!—no!   *(Shuddering)*
Not that! Not that!—I tell thee, holy man,
Thy raiments and thy ebony cross affright me!
Stand back! I have a crucifix myself,—
I have a crucifix! Methinks 'twere fitting
The deed—the vow—the symbol of the deed—
And the deed's register should tally, father!
            (Draws a cross-handled dagger, and raises it on high)
Behold the cross wherewith a vow like mine
Is written in Heaven!

MONK
                Thy words are madness, daughter,
And speak a purpose unholy—thy lips are livid—
Thine eyes are wild—tempt not the wrath divine!
Pause ere too late!—oh, be not—be not rash!
Swear not the oath—oh, swear it not!

LALAGE
                                    'Tis sworn!

116

III

An apartment in a Palace. POLITIAN *and* BALDAZZAR

BALDAZZAR

——Arouse thee now, Politian!
Thou must not—nay indeed, indeed, thou shalt not
Give away unto these humors. Be thyself!
Shake off the idle fancies that beset thee,
And live, for now thou diest!

POLITIAN

Not so, Baldazzar
Surely I live.

BALDAZZAR

Politian, it doth grieve me
To see thee thus.

POLITIAN

Baldazzar, it doth grieve me
To give thee cause for grief, my honored friend.
Command me, sir! what wouldst thou have me do?
At thy behest I will shake off that nature
Which from my forefathers I did inherit,
Which with my mother's milk I did imbibe,
And be no more Politian, but some other.
Command me, sir!

BALDAZZAR

To the field, then—to the field—
To the senate or the field.

POLITIAN

Alas! alas!
There is an imp would follow me even there!
There is an imp *hath* followed me even there!
There is—what voice was that?

BALDAZZAR

I heard it not.
I heard not any voice except thine own,
And the echo of thine own.

117

POLITIAN

Then I but dreamed.

BALDAZZAR

Give not thy soul to dreams: the camp—the court,
Befit thee—Fame awaits thee—Glory calls—
And her, the trumpet-tongued, thou wilt not hear
In hearkening to imaginary sounds
And phantom voices.

POLITIAN

It *is* a phantom voice!
Didst thou not hear it *then*?

BALDAZZAR

I heard it not.

POLITIAN

Thou heardst it not!—Baldazaar, speak no more
To me, Politian, of thy camps and courts.
Oh! I am sick, sick, sick, even unto death,
Of the hollow and high-sounding vanities
Of the populous Earth! Bear with me yet awhile!
We have been boys together—schoolfellows—
And now are friends—yet shall not be so long—
For in the eternal city thou shalt do me
A kind and gentle office, and a Power
A Power august, benignant and supreme—
Shall then absolve thee of all further duties
Unto thy friend.

BALDAZZAR

Thou speakest a fearful riddle
I *will* not understand.

POLITIAN

Yet now as Fate
Approaches, and the Hours are breathing low,
The sands of Time are changed to golden grains,
And dazzle me, Baldazzar. Alas! alas!
I *cannot* die, having within my heart
So keen a relish for the beautiful
As hath been kindled within it. Methinks the air
Is balmier now than it was wont to be—

118

Rich melodies are floating in the winds—
A rarer loveliness bedecks the earth—
And with a holier lustre the quiet moon
Sitteth in Heaven.—Hist! hist! thou canst not say
Thou hearest not *now*, Baldazzar?

BALDAZZAR
Indeed I hear not.

POLITIAN
Not hear it!—listen now!—listen!—the faintest sound
And yet the sweetest that ear ever heard!
A lady's voice!—and sorrow in the tone!
Baldazzar, it oppresses me like a spell!
Again!—again!—how solemnly it falls
Into my heart of hearts! that eloquent voice
Surely I never heard—yet it were well
Had I *but* heard it with its thrilling tones
In earlier days!

BALDAZZAR
I myself hear it now.
Be still!—the voice, if I mistake not greatly,
Proceeds from yonder lattice—which you may see
Very plainly through the window—it belongs,
Does it not? unto this palace of the Duke?
The singer is undoubtedly beneath
The roof of his Excellency—and perhaps
Is even that Alessandra of whom he spoke
As the betrothed of Castiglione,
His son and heir.

POLITIAN
Be still!—it comes again!

VOICE (*very faintly*)
"And is thy heart so strong
As for to leave me thus
Who hath loved thee so long
In wealth and woe among?
And is thy heart so strong
As for to leave me thus?
Say nay—say nay!"

119

BALDAZZAR

The song is English, and I oft have heard it
In merry England—never so plaintively—
Hist! hist! it comes again!

VOICE *(more loudly)*
"Is it so strong
As for to leave me thus
Who hath loved thee so long
In wealth and woe among?
And is thy heart so strong
As for to leave me thus?
Say nay—say nay!"

BALDAZZAR

'Tis hushed and all is still!

POLITIAN

All *is not* still!

BALDAZZAR

Let us go down.

POLITIAN

Go down, Baldazzar, go!

BALDAZZAR

The hour is growing late—the Duke awaits us,—
Thy presence is expected in the hall
Below. What ails thee, Earl Politian?

VOICE *(distinctly)*
"Who hath loved thee so long
In wealth and woe among,
And is thy heart so strong?
Say nay—say nay!"

BALDAZZAR

Let us descend—'tis time. Politian, give
These fancies to the wind. Remember, pray,
Your bearing lately savored much of rudeness
Unto the Duke. Arouse thee! and remember!

120

POLITIAN

Remember? I do. Lead on! I *do* remember.

(*Going*)

Let us descend. Believe me I would give,
Freely would give the broad lands of my earldom
To look upon the face hidden by yon lattice—
"To gaze upon that veiled face, and hear
Once more that silent tongue."

BALDAZZAR

Let me beg you, sir,
Descend with me—the Duke may be offended.
Let us go down, I pray you.

VOICE (*loudly*)
Say nay!—say nay!

POLITIAN (*aside*)

'Tis strange!—'tis very strange—methought the voice
Chimed in with my desires, and bade me stay!

(*Approaching the window*)

Sweet voice! I heed thee, and will surely stay.
Now be this Fancy, by Heaven! or be it Fate,
Still will I not descend. Baldazzar make
Apology unto the Duke for me;
I go not down to-night.

BALDAZZAR

Your lordship's pleasure
Shall be attended to. Good-night, Politian.

POLITIAN

Good-night, my friend, good-night.

IV

The gardens of a Palace—Moonlight

LALAGE *and* POLITIAN

LALAGE

And dost thou speak of love
To *me*, Politian?—dost thou speak of love

121

To Lalage?—ah, woe—ah, woe is me!
This mockery is most cruel—most cruel indeed!

POLITIAN

Weep not! oh, sob not thus!—thy bitter tears
Will madden me. Oh, mourn not, Lalage—
Be comforted! I know—I know it all,
And *still* I speak of love. Look at me, brightest
And beautiful Lalage!—turn here thine eyes!
Thou askest me if I could speak of love,
Knowing what I know, and seeing what I have seen.
Thou askest me that—and thus I answer thee—
Thus on my bended knee I answer thee.   *(Kneeling)*
Sweet Lalage, *I love thee—love thee—love thee;*
Thro' good and ill—thro' weal and woe I *love thee.*
Not mother, with her first-born on her knee,
Thrills with intenser love than I for thee.
Not on God's altar, in any time or clime,
Burned there a holier fire than burneth now
Within my spirit for *thee.* And do I love?   *(Arising)*
Even for thy woes I love thee—even for thy woes—
Thy beauty and thy woes.

LALAGE
Alas, proud Earl,
Thou dost forget thyself, remembering me!
How, in thy father's halls, among the maidens
Pure and reproachless of thy princely line,
Could the dishonored Lalage abide?
Thy wife, and with a tainted memory—
My seared and blighted name, how would it tally
With the ancestral honors of thy house,
And with thy glory?

POLITIAN
Speak not to me of glory!
I hate—I loathe the name; I do abhor
The unsatisfactory and ideal thing.
Art thou not Lalage and I Politian?
Do I not love—art thou not beautiful—
What need we more? Ha! glory!—now speak not of it.
By all I hold most sacred and most solemn—
By all my wishes now—my fears hereafter—

122

By all I scorn on earth and hope in heaven—
There is no deed I would more glory in,
Than in thy cause to scoff at this same glory
And trample it under foot. What matters it—
What matters it, my fairest, and my best,
That we go down unhonored and forgotten
Into the dust—so we descend together.
Descend together—and then—and then, perchance—

                    LALAGE
Why dost thou pause, Politian?

                    POLITIAN
                              And then, perchance
Arise together, Lalage, and roam
The starry and quiet dwellings of the blest,
And still—

                    LALAGE
          Why dost thou pause, Politian?

                    POLITIAN
And still *together—together*.

                    LALAGE
                    Now Earl of Leicester!
Thou *lovest* me, and in my heart of hearts
I feel thou lovest me truly.

                    POLITIAN
               Oh, Lalage!
                    (Throwing himself upon his knee)
And lovest thou *me*?

                    LALAGE
               Hist! hush! within the gloom
Of yonder trees methought a figure passed—
A spectral figure, solemn, and slow, and noiseless—
Like the grim shadow Conscience, solemn and noiseless.
                              (Walks across and returns)
I was mistaken—'twas but a giant bough
Stirred by the autumn wind. Politian!

123

POLITIAN

My Lalage—my love! why art thou moved?
Why dost thou turn so pale? Not Conscience' self,
Far less a shadow which thou likenest to it,
Should shake the firm spirit thus. But the night wind
Is chilly—and these melancholy boughs
Throw over all things a gloom.

LALAGE

Politian!
Thou speakest to me of love. Knowest thou the land
With which all tongues are busy—a land new found—
Miraculously found by one of Genoa—
A thousand leagues within the golden west?
A fairy land of flowers, and fruit, and sunshine,
And crystal lakes, and over-arching forests,
And mountains, around whose towering summits the winds
Of Heaven untrammelled flow—which air to breathe
Is Happiness now, and will be Freedom hereafter
In days that are to come?

POLITIAN

O, wilt thou—wilt thou
Fly to that Paradise—my Lalage, wilt thou
Fly thither with me? There Care shall be forgotten,
And Sorrow shall be no more, and Eros be all.
And life shall then be mine, for I will live
For thee, and in thine eyes—and thou shalt be
No more a mourner—but the radiant Joys
Shall wait upon thee, and the angel Hope
Attend thee ever; and I will kneel to thee
And worship thee, and call thee my beloved,
My own, my beautiful, my love, my wife,
My all;—oh, wilt thou—wilt thou, Lalage,
Fly thither with me?

LALAGE

A deed is to be done—
Castiglione lives!

POLITIAN

And he shall die!   (Exit)

124

LALAGE (*after a pause*)

And—he—shall—die!—alas!
Castiglione die? Who spoke the words?
Where am I?—what was it he said?—Politian!
Thou *art* not gone—thou are not *gone*, Politian!
I *feel* thou art not gone—yet dare not look,
Lest I behold thee not; thou *couldst* not go
With those words upon thy lips—O, speak to me!
And let me hear thy voice—one word—one word,
To say thou art not gone,—one little sentence,
To say how thou dost scorn—how thou dost hate
My womanly weakness. Ha! ha! thou *art* not gone—
O speak to me! I *knew* thou wouldst not go!
I knew thou wouldst not, couldst not, *durst* not go.
Villain, thou *art* not gone—thou mockest me!
And thus I clutch thee—thus!—He is gone, he is gone—
Gone—gone. Where am I?—'tis well—'tis very well!
So that the blade be keen—the blow be sure,
'Tis well, 'tis *very* well—alas! alas!

V

The suburbs. POLITIAN *alone*

POLITIAN

This weakness grows upon me. I am faint,
And much I fear me ill—it will not do
To die ere I have lived!—Stay, stay thy hand,
O Azrael, yet awhile!—Prince of the Powers
Of Darkness and the Tomb, O pity me!
O pity me! let me not perish now,
In the budding of my Paradisal Hope!
Give me to live yet—yet a little while:
'Tis I who pray for life—I who so late
Demanded but to die!—what sayeth the Count?
(*Enter* BALDAZZAR)

BALDAZZAR

That knowing no cause of quarrel or of feud
Between the Earl Politian and himself,
He doth decline your cartel.

125

POLITIAN

What didst thou say?
What answer was it you brought me, good Baldazzar?
With what excessive fragrance the zephyr comes
Laden from yonder bowers!—a fairer day,
Or one more worthy Italy, methinks
No mortal eyes have seen!—*what* said the Count?

BALDAZZAR

That he, Castiglione, not being aware
Of any feud existing, or any cause
Of quarrel between your lordship and himself,
Cannot accept the challenge.

POLITIAN

It is most true—
All this is very true. When saw you, sir,
When saw you now, Baldazzar, in the frigid
Ungenial Britain which we left so lately,
A heaven so calm as this—so utterly free
From the evil taint of clouds?—and he did *say*?

BALDAZZAR

No more, my lord, than I have told you, sir:
The Count Castiglione will not fight,
Having no cause for quarrel.

POLITIAN

Now this is true—
All very true. Thou art my friend, Baldazzar,
And I have not forgotten it—thou'lt do me
A piece of service; wilt thou go back and say
Unto this man, that I, the Earl of Leicester,
Hold him a villain?—thus much, I prythee, say
Unto the Count—it is exceeding just
He should have cause for quarrel.

BALDAZZAR

My lord!—my friend!—

POLITIAN (*aside*)

'Tis he!—he comes himself? (*aloud*) Thou reasonest well.
I know what thou wouldst say—not send the message—
Well!—I will think of it—I will not send it.

126

Now prythee, leave me—hither doth come a person
With whom affairs of a most private nature
I would adjust.

BALDAZZAR
I go—to-morrow we meet,
Do we not?—at the Vatican.

POLITIAN
At the Vatican.

(Exit BALDAZZAR)

Enter CASTIGLIONE

CASTIGLIONE
The Earl of Leicester here!

POLITIAN
I *am* the Earl of Leicester, and thou seest,
Dost thou not? that I am here.

CASTIGLIONE
My lord, some strange,
Some singular mistake—misunderstanding—
Hath without doubt arisen: thou hast been urged
Thereby, in heat of anger, to address
Some words most unaccountable, in writing,
To me, Castiglione; the bearer being
Baldazzar, Duke of Surrey. I am aware
Of nothing which might warrant thee in this thing,
Having given thee no offence. Ha!—am I right?
'Twas a mistake?—undoubtedly—we all
Do err at times.

POLITIAN
Draw, villain, and prate no more!

CASTIGLIONE
Ha!—draw?—and villain? have at thee then at once,
Proud Earl!

(Draws)

POLITIAN *(drawing)*
Thus to the expiatory tomb,
Untimely sepulchre, I do devote thee
In the name of Lalage!

127

CASTIGLIONE *(letting fall his sword and recoiling to the extremity of the stage)*
Of Lalage!
Hold off—thy sacred hand!—avaunt, I say!
Avaunt—I will not fight thee—indeed I dare not.

POLITIAN
Thou wilt not fight with me didst say, Sir Count?
Shall I be baffled thus?—now this is well;
Didst say thou *darest* not? Ha!

CASTIGLIONE
I dare not—dare not—
Hold off thy hand—with that beloved name
So fresh upon thy lips I will not fight thee—
I cannot—dare not.

POLITIAN
Now by my halidom
I do believe thee!—coward, I do believe thee!

CASTIGLIONE
Ha!—coward!—this may not be!
(Clutches his sword and staggers towards POLITIAN, *but his purpose is changed before reaching him, and he falls upon his knee at the feet of the Earl)*
Alas! my lord,
It is—it is—most true. In such a cause
I am the veriest coward. O pity me!

POLITIAN *(greatly softened)*
Alas!—I do—indeed I pity thee.

CASTIGLIONE
And Lalage—

POLITIAN
Scoundrel!—arise and die!

CASTIGLIONE
It needeth not be—thus—thus—O let me die
Thus on my bended knee. It were most fitting
That in this deep humiliation I perish.

128

For in the fight I will not raise a hand
Against thee, Earl of Leicester. Strike thou home—

(Baring his bosom)

Here is no let or hindrance to thy weapon—
Strike home. I *will not* fight thee.

POLITIAN

Now, s' Death and Hell!
Am I not—am I not sorely—grievously tempted
To take thee at thy word? But mark me, sir,
Think not to fly me thus. Do thou prepare
For public insult in the streets—before
The eyes of the citizens. I'll follow thee—
Like an avenging spirit I'll follow thee
Even unto death. Before those whom thou lovest—
Before all Rome I'll taunt thee, villain,—I'll taunt thee,
Dost hear? with *cowardice*—thou *will not* fight me?
Thou liest! thou *shalt!*

(Exit)

CASTIGLIONE

Now this indeed is just!
Most righteous, and most just, avenging Heaven!

129

To F——

Beloved! amid the earnest woes
   That crowd around my earthly path—
(Drear path, alas! where grows
Not even one lonely rose)—
   My soul at least a solace hath
In dreams of thee, and therein knows
An Eden of bland repose.

And thus thy memory is to me
   Like some enchanted far-off isle
In some tumultuous sea—
Some ocean throbbing far and free
   With storms—but where meanwhile
Serenest skies continually
   Just o'er that one bright island smile.

Hymn

At morn—at noon—at twilight dim—
Maria! thou hast heard my hymn!
In joy and woe—in good and ill—
Mother of God, be with me still!
When the hours flew brightly by,
And not a cloud obscured the sky,
My soul, lest it should truant be,
Thy grace did guide to thine and thee;
Now, when storms of Fate o'ercast
Darkly my Present and my Past,
Let my Future radiant shine
With sweet hopes of thee and thine!

The Conqueror Worm

Lo! 'tis a gala night
   Within the lonesome latter years!
An angel throng, bewinged, bedight
   In veils, and drowned in tears,
Sit in a theatre, to see
   A play of hopes and fears,
While the orchestra breathes fitfully
   The music of the spheres.

Mimes, in the form of God on high,
   Mutter and mumble low,
And hither and thither fly—
   Mere puppets they, who come and go
At bidding of vast formless things
   That shift the scenery to and fro,
Flapping from out their Condor wings
   Invisible Woe!

That motley drama—oh, be sure
   It shall not be forgot!
With its Phantom chased for evermore,
   By a crowd that seize it not,
Through a circle that ever returneth in
   To the self-same spot,
And much of Madness, and more of Sin,
   And Horror the soul of the plot.

But see, amid the mimic rout
   A crawling shape intrude!
A blood-red thing that writhes from out
   The scenic solitude!
It writhes!—it writhes!—with mortal pangs
   The mimes become its food,
And seraphs sob at vermin fangs
   In human gore imbued.

Out—out are the lights—out all!
   And, over each quivering form,
The curtain, a funeral pall,
   Comes down with the rush of a storm,
While the angels, all pallid and wan,
   Uprising, unveiling, affirm
That the play is the tragedy, "Man,"
   And its hero the Conqueror Worm.

The Coliseum

Type of the antique Rome! Rich reliquary
Of lofty contemplation left to Time
By buried centuries of pomp and power!
At length—at length—after so many days
Of weary pilgrimage and burning thirst,
(Thirst for the springs of lore that in thee lie,)
I kneel, an altered and an humble man,
Amid thy shadows, and so drink within
My very soul thy grandeur, gloom, and glory!

Vastness! and Age! and Memories of Eld!
Silence! and Desolation! and dim Night!
I feel ye now—I feel ye in your strength—
O spells more sure than e'er Judaean king
Taught in the gardens of Gethsemane!
O charms more potent than the rapt Chaldee
Ever drew down from out the quiet stars!

Here, where a hero fell, a column falls!
Here, where the mimic eagle glared in gold,
A midnight vigil holds the swarthy bat!
Here, where the dames of Rome their gilded hair
Waved to the wind, now wave the reed and thistle!
Here, where on golden throne the monarch lolled,
Glides, spectre-like, unto his marble home,
Lit by the wan light of the hornèd moon,
The swift and silent lizard of the stones!

But stay! these walls—these ivy-clad arcades—
These moldering plinths—these sad and blackened shafts—
These vague entablatures—this crumbling frieze—
These shattered cornices—this wreck—this ruin—
These stones—alas! these grey stones—are they all—
All of the famed, and the colossal left
By the corrosive Hours to Fate and me?

"Not all"—the Echoes answer me—"not all!
Prophetic sounds and loud, arise forever
From us, and from all Ruin, unto the wise,
As melody from Memnon to the Sun.
We rule the hearts of mightiest men—we rule
With a despotic sway all giant minds.
We are not impotent—we pallid stones.
Not all our power is gone—not all our fame—

THE COLISEUM

Not all the magic of our high renown—
Not all the wonder that encircles us—
Not all the mysteries that in us lie—
Not all the memories that hang upon
And cling around about us as a garment,
Clothing us in a robe of more than glory."

Eulalie

I dwelt alone
In a world of moan,
And my soul was a stagnant tide,
Till the fair and gentle Eulalie became my blushing bride—
Till the yellow-haired young Eulalie became my smiling bride.

Ah, less—less bright
The stars of the night
Than the eyes of the radiant girl!
And never a flake
That the vapor can make
With the moon-tints of purple and pearl,
Can vie with the modest Eulalie's most unregarded curl—
Can compare with the bright-eyed Eulalie's most humble and careless
  curl.

Now Doubt—now Pain
Come never again,
For her soul gives me sigh for sigh,
And all day long
Shines, bright and strong,
Astarté within the sky,
While ever to her dear Eulalie upturns her matron eye—
While ever to her young Eulalie upturns her violet eye.

Dreamland

By a route obscure and lonely,
Haunted by ill angels only,
Where an Eidolon, named NIGHT,
On a black throne reigns upright,
I have reached these lands but newly
From an ultimate dim Thule—
From a wild clime that lieth, sublime,
    Out of SPACE—out of TIME.

Bottomless vales and boundless floods,
And chasms, and caves, and Titan woods,
With forms that no man can discover
For the tears that drip all over;
Mountains toppling evermore
Into seas without a shore;
Seas that restlessly aspire,
Surging, unto skies of fire;
Lakes that endlessly outspread
Their lone waters—lone and dead,—
Their still waters—still and chilly
With the snows of the lolling lily.

By the lakes that thus outspread
Their lone waters, lone and dead,—
Their sad waters, sad and chilly
With the snows of the lolling lily,—
By the mountains—near the river
Murmuring lowly, murmuring ever,—
By the grey woods,—by the swamp
Where the toad and the newt encamp,—
By the dismal tarns and pools
    Where dwell the Ghouls,—
By each spot the most unholy—
In each nook most melancholy,—
There the traveller meets aghast
Sheeted Memories of the Past—
Shrouded forms that start and sigh
As they pass the wanderer by—
White-robed forms of friends long given,
In agony, to the Earth—and Heaven.

DREAMLAND

For the heart whose woes are legion
'Tis a peaceful, soothing region—
For the spirit that walks in shadow
'Tis—oh, 'tis an Eldorado!
But the traveller, travelling through it,
May not—dare not openly view it!
Never its mysteries are exposed
To the weak human eye unclosed;
So wills its King, who hath forbid
The uplifting of the fringèd lid;
And thus the sad Soul that here passes
Beholds it but through darkened glasses.

By a route obscure and lonely,
Haunted by ill angels only,
Where an Eidolon, named NIGHT,
On a black throne reigns upright,
I have wandered home but newly
From this ultimate dim Thule.

To F——s S. O——d

Thou wouldst be loved?—then let thy heart
    From its present pathway part not!
Being everything which now thou art,
    Be nothing which thou art not.
So with the world thy gentle ways,
    Thy grace, thy more than beauty,
Shall be an endless theme of praise,
    And love—a simple duty.

Sonnet—To Zante

Fair isle, that from the fairest of all flowers,
    Thy gentlest of all gentle names dost take!
How many memories of what radiant hours
    At sight of thee and thine at once awake!
How many scenes of what departed bliss!
    How many thoughts of what entombèd hopes!
How many visions of a maiden that is
    No more—no more upon thy verdant slopes!
No more! alas, that magical sad sound
    Transforming all! Thy charms shall please *no more*—
Thy memory *no more!* Accursèd ground
    Henceforth I hold thy flower-enameled shore,
O hyacinthine isle! O purple Zante!
      "Isola d'oro! Fior di Levante!"

TO ZANTE

Sonnet—Silence

There are some qualities—some incorporate things,
   That have a double life, which thus is made
A type of that twin entity which springs
   From matter and light, evinced in solid and shade.
There is a two-fold *Silence*—sea and shore—
   Body and soul. One dwells in lonely places,
   Newly with grass o'ergrown; some solemn graces,
Some human memories and tearful lore,
Render him terrorless: his name's "No More."
He is the corporate Silence: dread him not!
   No power hath he of evil in himself;
But should some urgent fate (untimely lot!)
   Bring thee to meet his shadow (nameless elf,
That haunteth the lone regions where hath trod
No foot of man,) commend thyself to God!

The Poems of Edgar Allan Poe

VII

THE RATIONALE OF VERSE

[AN ESSAY]

"THE RATIONALE OF VERSE," revised from a tentative "Notes on English Verse," promises to deal profoundly with the intricacies of versification. Poe proposes to use the word "verse" to cover a consideration of rhythm, rhyme and metre "without pedantry." The long and tortuous essay scarcely lives up to its promise. It is not only pedantic but inaccurate.

Poe's attempts to impose new laws on metre are futile because they are founded on a false theory, the theory that English versification is based on "long" and "short" syllables. English verse, unlike Latin, is not based on quantity but on accent, on the disposition of stress. And Poe, piling one incorrect example upon another, accomplishes little more than a series of tiresome examples and tedious misconceptions.

The most valuable, and perhaps the only interesting, parts of Poe's essay on "The Rationale of Verse" are his vagaries. His elaborate schemes of notation and emphasis may be arbitrary, but his passion for poetry is always there. Almost submerged by Poe's crotchets about the "astrologos," the "bastard iambus," the "quick trochee," and the "prosodial schools," the poet's passion struggles through. No amount of pedantic dead weight can drown it.

The Rationale of Verse

THE WORD "Verse" is here used not in its strict or primitive sense, but as the term most convenient for expressing generally and without pedantry all that is involved in the consideration of rhythm, rhyme, metre, and versification.

There is, perhaps, no topic in polite literature which has been more pertinaciously discussed, and there is certainly not one about which so much inaccuracy, confusion, misconception, misrepresentation, mystification, and downright ignorance on all sides, can be fairly said to exist. Were the topic really difficult, or did it lie, even, in the cloud-land of metaphysics, where the doubt-vapors may be made to assume any and every shape at the will or at the fancy of the gazer, we should have less reason to wonder at all this contradiction and perplexity; but in fact the subject is exceedingly simple; one-tenth of it, possibly, may be called ethical; nine-tenths, however, appertain to mathematics; and the whole is included within the limits of the commonest common-sense.

"But, if this is the case, how," it will be asked, "can so much misunderstanding have arisen? Is it conceivable that a thousand profound scholars, investigating so very simple a matter for centuries, have not been able to place it in the fullest light, at least, of which it is susceptible?" These queries, I confess, are not easily answered:—at all events, a satisfactory reply to them might cost more trouble, than would, if properly considered, the whole *vexata quaestio* to which they have reference. Nevertheless, there is little difficulty or danger in suggesting that the "thousand profound scholars" *may* have failed, first, because they were scholars, secondly, because they were profound, and thirdly, because they were a thousand—the impotency of the scholarship and profundity having been thus multiplied a thousand-fold. I am serious in these suggestions; for, first again, there is something in "scholarship" which seduces us into blind worship of Bacon's Idol of the Theatre—into irrational deference to antiquity; secondly, the proper "profundity" is rarely profound—it is the nature of truth in general, as of some ores in particular, to be richest when most superficial; thirdly, the clearest subject may be overclouded by mere superabundance of talk. In chemistry, the best way of separating two bodies is to add a third; in speculation, fact often agrees with fact and argument with argument, until an additional well-meaning fact or argument sets everything by the ears. In one case out of a hundred a point is excessively discussed because it is obscure; in the ninety-nine remaining it is obscure because excessively discussed. When a topic is thus circumstanced, the readiest mode of investigating it is to forget that any previous investigation has been attempted.

But, in fact, while much has been written on the Greek and Latin rhythms, and even on the Hebrew, little effort has been made at ex-

147

amining that of any of the modern tongues. As regards the English, comparatively nothing has been done. It may be said, indeed, that we are without a treatise on our own verse. In our ordinary grammars and in our works, on rhetoric or prosody in general, may be found occasional chapters, it is true, which have the heading "Versification," but these are, in all instances, exceedingly meagre. They pretend to no analysis; they propose nothing like system; they make no attempt at even rule; everything depends upon "authority." They are confined, in fact, to mere exemplification of the supposed varieties of English feet and English lines;—although in no work with which I am acquainted are these feet correctly given or these lines detailed in anything like their full extent. Yet what has been mentioned is all— if we except the occasional introduction of some pedagogism, such as this, borrowed from the Greek Prosodies: "When a syllable is wanting, the verse is said to be catalectic; when the measure is exact, the line is acatalectic; when there is a redundant syllable it forms hypermeter." Now whether a line be termed catalectic or acatalectic is, perhaps, a point of no vital importance; it is even possible that the student may be able to decide, promptly, when the *a* should be employed and when omitted, yet be incognizant, at the same time, of *all* that is worth knowing in regard to the structure of verse.

A leading defect in each of our treatises (if treatises they can be called), is the confining the subject to mere *Versification*, while *Verse* in general, with the understanding given to the term in the heading of this paper, is the real question at issue. Nor am I aware of even one of our grammars which so much as properly defines the word versification itself. "Versification," says a work now before me, of which the accuracy is far more than usual—the "English Grammar" of Goold Brown,—"Versification is the art of arranging words into lines of correspondent length, so as to produce harmony by the regular alternation of syllables differing in quantity." The commencement of this definition might apply, indeed, to the *art* of versification, but not versification itself. Versification is not the art of arranging, &c., but the actual arranging—a distinction too obvious to need comment. The error here is identical with one which has been too long permitted to disgrace the initial page of every one of our school grammars. I allude to the definitions of English grammar itself. "English grammar," it is said, "is the art of speaking and writing the English language correctly." This phraseology, or something essentially similar, is employed, I believe, by Bacon, Miller, Fisk, Greenleaf, Ingersoll, Kirkland, Cooper, Flint, Pue, Comly, and many others. These gentlemen, it is presumed, adopted it without examination from Murray, who derived it from Lily (whose work was "*quam solam Regia Majestas in omnibus scholis docendam praecipit*"), and who appropriated it without acknowledgment, but with some unimportant modification, from the Latin Grammar of Leonicenus. It may be shown, however, that this definition, so complacently received, is not, and cannot be, a proper definition of English grammar. A definition is that which so describes its object as to distinguish it from all others; it is no definition of any one thing if its terms are applicable to any one other. But if it be asked: "What is the design—the end—the aim of English grammar?" our obvious answer is: "The art of speaking and writing the English language correctly,"—that is to say, we must use the precise words employed as the definition of English grammar itself. But the object to be attained by any means is, assuredly, not the means. English grammar and the end contemplated by English grammar are two matters sufficiently distinct; nor can the one be more reasonably regarded as the other than a fishing-hook as a fish. The definition, therefore, which is applicable in the latter instance, *cannot*, in the former, be true. Grammar in general is the analysis of language; English Grammar of the English.

But to return to Versification as defined in our extract above. "It is the art," says the extract, "of arranging words into lines *of correspondent length*." Not so; a correspondence in the length of lines is by no means essential. Pindaric odes are, surely, instances of versification, yet these compositions are noted for extreme diversity in the length of their lines.

The arrangement is, moreover, said to be for the purpose of producing "*harmony* by the regular alternation," &c. But *harmony* is not the sole aim—not even the principal one. In the construction of verse, *melody* should never be left out of view; yet this is a point which all our prosodies have most unaccountably forborne to touch. Reasoned rules on this topic should form a portion of all systems of rhythm.

"So as to produce harmony," says the definition, "by the *regular alternation*," &c. A *regular* alternation, as described, forms no part of any principle of versification. The arrangement of spondees and dactyls, for example, in the Greek hexameter, is an arrangement which may be termed *at random*. At least it is arbitrary. Without interference with the line as a whole, a dactyl may be substituted for a spondee, or the converse, at any point other than the ultimate and penultimate feet, of which the former is always a spondee, the latter nearly always a dactyl. Here, it is clear, we have no "*regular* alternation of syllables differing in quantity."

"So as to produce harmony," proceeds the definition, "by the regular alternation of *syllables differing in quantity*,"—in other words, by the alternation of long and short syllables; for in rhythm all syllables are necessarily either short or long. But not only do I

149

deny the necessity of any *regularity* in the succession of feet and, by consequence, of syllables, but dispute the essentiality of any *alternation,* regular or irregular, of syllables long and short. Our author, observe, is now engaged in a definition of versification in general, not of English versification in particular. But the Greek and Latin metres abound in the spondee and pyrrhic—the former consisting of two long syllables, the latter of two short; and there are innumerable instances of the immediate succession of many spondees and many pyrrhics.

Here is a passage from Silius Italicus:

> Fallis te, mensas inter quod credis inermem
> Tot bellis quaesita viro, tot caedibus armat
> Majestas eterna ducem: si admoveris ora
> Cannas, et Trebium ante oculos, Trasymenaque busta,
> Et Pauli stare ingentem miraberis umbram.

Making the elisions demanded by the classic prosodies, we should scan these hexameters thus:

> *Fallis* | *te men* | *sas in* | *ter quod* | *cre*dis in | *ermem* |
> *Tot bel* | *lis quae* | *sit*a vi | *ro tot* | caedibus | *armat* |
> *Majes* | *tas e* | *ter*na du | *cem s'ad* | *moveris* | *ora* |
> *Cannas* | *et* Trebi' | *ant'* ocu | *los* Trasy | *men*aque | *busta* |
> Et *Pau* | *li sta* | *r' ingen* | *tem mi* | *ra*beris | *umbram* |

It will be seen that, in the first and last of these lines, we have only two short syllables in thirteen, with an uninterrupted succession of no less than *nine* long syllables. But how are we to reconcile all this with a definition of versification which describes it as "the art of arranging words into lines of correspondent length so as to produce harmony by the *regular alternation of syllables differing in quantity*"?

It may be urged, however, that our prosodist's *intention* was to speak of the English metres alone, and that, by omitting all mention of the spondee and pyrrhic, he has virtually avowed their exclusion from our rhythms. A grammarian is never excusable on the ground of good intentions. We demand from him, if from any one, rigorous precision of style. But grant the design. Let us admit that our author, following the example of all authors on English Prosody, has, in defining versification at large, intended a definition merely of the English. All these prosodists, we will say, reject the spondee and pyrrhic. Still all admit the iambus, which consists of a short syllable followed by a long; the trochee, which is the converse of the iambus; the dactyl, formed of one long syllable followed by two short; and the anapaest —two short succeeded by a long. The spondee is improperly rejected, as I shall presently show. The pyrrhic is rightfully dismissed. Its existence in either ancient or modern rhythm is purely chimerical, and the insisting on so perplexing a nonentity as a foot of *two short* syllables, affords, perhaps, the best evidence of the gross irrationality and subservience to authority which characterize our Prosody. In the meantime the acknowledged dactyl and anapaest are enough to sustain my proposition about the "alternation," &c., without reference to feet which are assumed to exist in the Greek and Latin metres alone: for an anapaest and a dactyl may meet in the same line; when, of course, we shall have an uninterrupted succession of four short syllables. The meeting of these two feet, to be sure, is an accident not contemplated in the definition now discussed; for this definition, in demanding a "regular alternation of syllables differing in quantity," insists on a regular succession of similar *feet*. But here is an example:

 Sing to me | Isa*belle.*

This is the opening line of a little ballad now before me, which proceeds in the same rhythm—a peculiarly beautiful one. More than all this: English lines are often well composed, entirely, of a regular succession of syllables *all of the same quantity*—the first lines, for instance, of the following quatrain by Arthur C. Coxe:

 March! march! march!
Making sounds as they tread.
Ho! ho! how they step,
Going down to the dead!

The line italicized is formed of three caesuras. The caesura, of which I have much to say hereafter, is rejected by the English Prosodies and grossly misrepresented in the classic. It is a perfect foot— the most important in all verse—and consists of a single *long* syllable; *but the length of this syllable varies.*

It has thus been made evident that there is *not one* point of the definition in question which does not involve an error. And for anything more satisfactory or more intelligible we shall look in vain to any published treatise on the topic.

So general and so total a failure can be referred only to radical misconception. In fact the English Prosodists have blindly followed the pedants. These latter, like *les moutons de Panurge,* have been occupied in incessant tumbling into ditches, for the excellent reason that their leaders have so tumbled before. The Iliad, being taken as a starting point, was made to stand instead of Nature and commonsense. Upon this poem, in place of facts and deduction from fact, or from natural law, were built systems of feet, metres, rhythms, rules, —rules that contradict each other every five minutes, and for nearly all of which there may be found twice as many exceptions as exam-

151

ples. If any one has a fancy to be thoroughly confounded—to see how far the infatuation of what is termed "classical scholarship" can lead a book-worm in the manufacture of darkness out of sunshine, let him turn over, for a few moments, any of the German Greek prosodies. The only thing clearly made out in them is a very magnificent contempt for Liebnitz' principle of "a sufficient reason."

To divert attention from the real matter in hand by any farther reference to these works, is unnecessary, and would be weak. I cannot call to mind, at this moment, one essential particular of information that is to be gleaned from them; and I will drop them here with merely this one observation: that, employing from among the numerous *"ancient"* feet the spondee, the trochee, the iambus, the anapaest, the dactyl, and the caesura alone, I will engage to scan *correctly* any of the Horatian rhythms, or any true rhythm that human ingenuity can conceive. And this excess of chimerical feet is, perhaps, the very least of the scholastic supererogations. *Ex uno disce omnia.* The fact is that *Quantity* is a point in whose investigation the lumber of mere learning may be dispensed with, if ever in any. Its appreciation is universal. It appertains to no region, nor race, nor era in especial. To melody and to harmony the Greeks hearkened with ears precisely similar to those which we employ for similar purposes at present; and I should not be condemned for heresy in asserting that a pendulum at Athens would have vibrated much after the same fashion as does a pendulum in the city of Penn.

Verse originates in the human enjoyment of equality, fitness. To this enjoyment, also, all the moods of verse—rhythm, metre, stanza, rhyme, alliteration, the *refrain,* and other analogous effects—are to be referred. As there are some readers who habitually confound rhythm and metre, it may be as well here to say that the former concerns the *character* of feet (that is, the arrangements of syllables) while the latter has to do with the *number* of these feet. Thus, by "a dactylic *rhythm*" we express a sequence of dactyls. By "a dactylic hexa*meter*" we imply a line or measure consisting of six of these dactyls.

To return to *equality.* Its idea embraces those of similarity, proportion, identity, repetition, and adaptation or fitness. It might not be very difficult to go even behind the idea of equality, and show both how and why it is that the human nature takes pleasure in it, but such an investigation would, for any purpose now in view, be supererogatory. It is sufficient that the *fact* is undeniable—the fact that man derives enjoyment from his perception of equality. Let us examine a crystal. We are at once interested by the equality between the sides and between the angles of one of its faces: the equality of the sides pleases us; that of the angles doubles the pleasure. On bringing to view a second face in all respects similar to the first, this pleasure seems to be squared; on bringing to view a third, it appears to be cubed, and so on. I have no doubt, indeed, that the delight experienced, if measurable, would be found to have exact mathematical relations such as I suggest; that is to say, as far as a certain point, beyond which there would be a decrease in similar relations.

The perception of pleasure in the equality of *sounds* is the principle of *Music*. Unpractised ears can appreciate only simple equalities, such as are found in ballad airs. While comparing one simple sound with another they are too much occupied to be capable of comparing the equality subsisting between these two simple sounds, taken conjointly, and two other similar simple sounds, taken conjointly. Practised ears, on the other hand, appreciate both equalities at the same instant—although it is absurd to suppose that both are *heard* at the same instant. One is heard and appreciated from itself: the other is heard by the memory; and the instant glides into and is confounded with the secondary, appreciation. Highly cultivated musical taste in this manner enjoys not only these double equalities, all appreciated at once, but takes pleasurable cognizance, through memory, of equalities the members of which occur at intervals so great that the uncultivated taste loses them altogether. That this latter can properly estimate or decide on the merits of what is called scientific music, is of course impossible. But scientific music has no claim to intrinsic excellence—it is fit for scientific ears alone. In its excess it is the triumph of the *physique* over the *morale* of music. The sentiment is overwhelmed by the sense. On the whole, the advocates of the simpler melody and harmony have infinitely the best of the argument; although there has been very little of real argument on the subject.

In *verse*, which cannot be better designated than as an inferior or less capable Music, there is, happily, little chance for perplexity. Its rigidly simple character not even Science—not even Pedantry can greatly pervert.

The rudiment of verse may, possibly, be found in the *spondee*. The very germ of a thought seeking satisfaction in equality of sound would result in the construction of words of two syllables, equally accented. In corroboration of this idea we find that spondees most abound in the most ancient tongues. The second step we can easily suppose to be the comparison, that is to say, the collocation, of two spondees—of two words composed each of a spondee. The third step would be the juxtaposition of three of these words. By this time the perception of monotone would induce farther consideration: and thus arises what Leigh Hunt so flounders in discussing under the title of "The *Principle* of Variety in Uniformity." Of course there is no principle in the case—nor in maintaining it. The "Uniformity" is the

153

principle; the "Variety" is but the principle's natural safeguard from self-destruction by excess of self. "Uniformity," besides, is the very worst word that could have been chosen for the expression of the *general* idea at which it aims.

The perception of monotone having given rise to an attempt at its relief, the first thought in this new direction would be that of collating two or more words formed each of two syllables differently accented (that is to say, short and long) but having the same order in each word, —in other terms, of collating two or more iambuses, or two or more trochees. And here let me pause to assert that more pitiable nonsense has been written on the topic of *long* and *short* syllables than on any other subject under the sun. In general, a syllable is long or short, just as it is difficult or easy of enunciation. The *natural* long syllables are those encumbered—the *natural* short syllables are those *un*encumbered, with consonants; all the rest is mere artificiality and jargon. The Latin Prosodies have a rule that "a vowel before two consonants is long." This rule is deduced from "authority"—that is, from the observation that vowels so circumstanced, in the ancient poems, are always in syllables long by the laws of scansion. The philosophy of the rule is untouched, and lies simply in the physical difficulty of giving voice to such syllables—of performing the lingual evolutions necessary for their utterance. Of course, it is not the *vowel* that is long (although the rule says so), but the syllable of which the vowel is a part. It will be seen that the length of a syllable, depending on the facility or difficulty of its enunciation, must have great variation in various syllables; but for the purposes of verse we suppose a long syllable equal to two short ones:—and the natural deviation from this relativeness we correct in perusal. The more closely our long syllables approach this relation with our short ones, the better, *ceteris paribus,* will be our verse: but if the relation does not exist of itself, we force it by emphasis, which can, of course, make any syllable as long as desired;—or, by an effort we can pronounce with unnatural brevity a syllable that is naturally too long. *Accented* syllables are of course always long—but, where *un*encumbered with consonants, must be classed among the *unnaturally* long. Mere custom has declared that we shall accent them—that is to say, dwell upon them; but no inevitable lingual difficulty forces us to do so. In fine, every long syllable must of its own accord occupy in its utterance, or must be *made* to occupy, precisely the time demanded for two short ones. The only exception to this rule is found in the caesura—of which more anon.

The success of the experiment with the trochees or iambuses (the one would have suggested the other) must have led to a trial of dactyls or anapaests—natural dactyls or anapaests—dactyls or anapaestic *words.* And now some degree of complexity has been attained. There

154

is an appreciation, first, of the equality between the several dactyls, or anapaests, and, secondly, of that between the long syllable and the two short conjointly. But here it may be said that step after step would have been taken, in continuation of this routine, until all the feet of the Greek Prosodies became exhausted. Not so; these remaining feet have no existence except in the brains of the scholiasts. It is needless to imagine men inventing these things, and folly to explain how and why they invented them, until it shall be first shown that they are actually invented. All other "feet" than those which I have specified, are, if not impossible at first view, merely combinations of the specified; and, although this assertion is rigidly true, I will, to avoid misunderstanding, put it in a somewhat different shape. I will say, then, that at present I am aware of no *rhythm*—nor do I believe that any one can be constructed—which, in its last analysis, will not be found to consist altogether of the feet I have mentioned, either existing in their individual and obvious condition, or interwoven with each other in accordance with simple natural laws which I will endeavor to point out hereafter.

We have now gone so far as to suppose men constructing indefinite sequences of spondaic, iambic, trochaic, dactylic, or anapaestic words. In *extending* these sequences, they would be again arrested by the sense of monotone. A succession of spondees would *immediately* have displeased; one of iambuses or of trochees, on account of the variety included within the foot itself, would have taken longer to displease; one of dactyls or anapaests, still longer; but even the last, if extended very far, must have become wearisome. The idea, first, of curtailing, and, secondly, of defining the length of, a sequence, would thus at once have arisen. Here then is the *line*, or verse proper.* The principle of equality being constantly at the bottom of the whole process, lines would naturally be made, in the first instance, equal in the number of their feet; in the second instance, there would be variation in the mere number: one line would be twice as long as another; then one would be some less obvious multiple of another; then still less obvious proportions would be adopted;—nevertheless there would be *proportion*, that is to say, a phase of equality, still.

Lines being once introduced, the necessity of distinctly defining these lines *to the ear*, (as yet written verse does not exist,) would lead to a scrutiny of their capabilities *at their terminations:*—and now would spring up the idea of equality in sound between the final syllables—in other words, of *rhyme*. First, it would be used only in the

---

*Verse, from the Latin *vertere*, to turn, is so called on account of the turning or re-commencement of the series of feet. Thus a verse, strictly speaking, is a line. In this sense, however, I have preferred using the latter word alone; employing the former in the general acceptation given it in the heading of this paper.

iambic, anapaestic, and spondaic rhythms (granting that the latter had not been thrown aside, long since, on account of its tameness), because in these rhythms, the concluding syllable being long, could best sustain the necessary protraction of the voice. No great while could elapse, however, before the effect, found pleasant as well as useful, would be applied to the two remaining rhythms. But as the chief force of rhyme must lie in the accented syllable, the attempt to create rhyme at all in these two remaining rhythms, the trochaic and dactylic, would necessarily result in double and triple rhymes, such as *beauty* with *duty* (trochaic) and *beautiful* with *dutiful* (dactylic).

It must be observed, that in suggesting these processes, I assign them no date; nor do I even insist upon their order. Rhyme is supposed to be of modern origin, and were this proved, my positions remain untouched. I may say, however, in passing, that several instances of rhyme occur in the "Clouds" of Aristophanes, and that the Roman poets occasionally employ it. There is an effective species of ancient rhyming which has never descended to the moderns: that in which the ultimate and penultimate syllables rhyme with each other. For example:

Parturiunt montes; nascetur ridicu*lus mus.*

And again:

Litoreis ingens inventa sub ilici*bus sus.*

The terminations of Hebrew verse (as far as understood) show no signs of rhyme; but what thinking person can doubt that it did actually exist? That men have so obstinately and blindly insisted, *in general,* even up to the present day, in confining rhyme to the *ends* of lines, when its effect is even better applicable elsewhere, intimates, in my opinion, the sense of some *necessity* in the connection of the end with the rhyme,—hints that the origin of rhyme lay in a necessity which connected it with the end,—shows that neither mere accident nor mere fancy gave rise to the connection,—points, in a word, at the very necessity which I have suggested (that of some mode of defining lines *to the ear*) as the true origin of rhyme. Admit this, and we throw the origin far back in the night of Time—beyond the origin of written verse.

But, to resume. The amount of complexity I have now supposed to be attained is very considerable. Various systems of equalization are appreciated at once (or nearly so) in their respective values and in the value of each system with reference to all the others. As our present *ultimatum* of complexity, we have arrived at triple-rhymed, natural-dactylic lines, existing proportionally as well as equally with regard to other triple-rhymed, natural-dactylic lines. For example:

> Virginal Lilian, rigidly, humblily dutiful;
> Saintlily, lowlily,
> Thrillingly, holily
> Beautiful!

Here we appreciate, first, the absolute equality between the long syllable of each dactyl and the two short conjointly; secondly, the absolute equality between each dactyl and any other dactyl—in other words, among all the dactyls; thirdly, the absolute equality between the two middle lines; fourthly, the absolute equality between the first line and the three others taken conjointly; fifthly, the absolute equality between the last two syllables of the respective words "dutiful" and "beautiful"; sixthly, the absolute equality between the two last syllables of the respective words "lowlily" and "holily"; seventhly, the proximate equality between the first syllable of "dutiful" and the first syllable of "beautiful"; eighthly, the proximate equality between the first syllable of "lowlily" and that of "holily"; ninthly, the proportional equality (that of five to one) between the first line and each of its members, the dactyls; tenthly, the proportional equality (that of two to one,) between each of the middle lines and its members, the dactyls; eleventhly, the proportional equality between the first line and each of the two middle—that of five to two; twelfthly, the proportional equality between the first line and the last—that of five to one; thirteenthly, the proportional equality between each of the middle lines and the last—that of two to one; lastly, the proportional equality, as concerns number, between all the lines, taken collectively, and any individual line—that of four to one.

The consideration of this last equality would give birth immediately to the idea of *stanza**—that is to say, the insulation of lines into equal or obviously proportional masses. In its primitive (which was also its best) form, the stanza would most probably have had absolute unity. In other words, the removal of any one of its lines would have rendered it imperfect; as in the case above, where, if the last line, for example, be taken away, there is left no rhyme to the "dutiful" of the first. Modern stanza is excessively loose—and where so, ineffective, as a matter of course.

Now, although in the deliberate written statement which I have here given of these various systems of equalities, there seems to be an infinity of complexity—so much that it is hard to conceive the mind taking cognizance of them all in the brief period occupied by the perusal or recital of the stanza—yet the difficulty is in fact apparent only when we will it to become so. Any one fond of mental experiment may satisfy himself, by trial, that, in listening to the lines, he

---

*A stanza is often vulgarly, and with gross impropriety, called a *verse*.

157

does actually (although with a seeming unconsciousness, on account of the rapid evolutions of sensation) recognize and instantaneously appreciate (more or less intensely as his ear is cultivated) each and all of the equalizations detailed. The pleasure received, or receivable, has very much such progressive increase, and in very nearly such mathematical relations, as those which I have suggested in the case of the crystal.

It will be observed that I speak of merely a proximate equality between the first syllable of "dutiful" and that of "beautiful"; and it may be asked why we cannot imagine the earliest rhymes to have had absolute instead of proximate equality of sound. But absolute equality would have involved the use of identical words; and it is the duplicate sameness or monotony—that of sense as well as that of sound—which would have caused these rhymes to be rejected in the very first instance.

The narrowness of the limits within which verse composed of natural feet alone must necessarily have been confined, would have led, after a *very* brief interval, to the trial and immediate adoption of artificial feet—that is to say, of feet *not* constituted each of a single word, but two or even three words; or of parts of words. These feet would be intermingled with natural ones. For example:

a *breath* | can *make* | them *as* | a *breath* | has *made*.

This is an iambic line in which each iambus is formed of two words. Again:

The *un* | im*a* | gin*a* | ble *might* | of *Jove*.

This is an iambic line in which the first foot is formed of a word and a part of a word; the second and third, of parts taken from the body or interior of a word; the fourth, of a part and a whole; the fifth, of two complete words. There are no *natural* feet in either lines. Again:

Can it be | *fan*cied that | *Dei*ty | *ev*er vin | *dic*tively
Made in his | *im*age a | *man*nikin | *mere*ly to | *mad*den it?

These are two dactylic lines in which we find natural feet ("Deity," "mannikin"), feet composed of two words ("fancied that," "image a," "merely to," "madden it"), feet composed of three words ("can it be," "made in his"), a foot composed of a part of a word ("dictively"), and a foot composed of a word and a part of a word ("ever vin").

And now, in our supposititious progress, we have gone so far as to exhaust all the *essentialities* of verse. What follows may, strictly speaking, be regarded as embellishment merely—but even in this embellishment, the rudimental sense of *equality* would have been the never-ceasing impulse. It would, for example, be simply in seeking farther administration to this sense that men would come, in time, to think of the *refrain*, or burden, where, at the closes of the several stanzas of a poem, one word or phrase is *repeated;* and of alliteration, in whose simplest form a consonant is *repeated* in the commencements of various words. This effect would be extended so as to embrace repetitions both of vowels and of consonants, in the bodies as well as in the beginnings of words; and, at a later period would be made to infringe on the province of rhyme, by the introduction of general similarity of sound between whole feet occurring in the body of a line:—all of which modifications I have exemplified in the line above.

*M*ade in his i*m*age a *mannikin m*erely to *madden it.*

Farther cultivation would improve also the *refrain* by relieving its monotone in slightly varying the phrase at each repetition, or (as I have attempted to do in "The Raven") in retaining the phrase and varying its application—although this latter point is not strictly a rhythmical effect *alone.* Finally, poets when fairly wearied with following precedent—following it the more closely the less they perceived it in company with Reason—would adventure so far as to indulge in positive rhyme at other points than the ends of lines. First, they would put it in the middle of the line; then at some point where the multiple would be less obvious; then, alarmed at their own audacity, they would undo all their work by cutting these lines in two. And here is the fruitful source of the infinity of "short metre," by which modern poetry, if not distinguished, is at least disgraced. It would require a high degree, indeed, both of cultivation and of courage, on the part of any versifier, to enable him to place his rhymes—and let them remain—at unquestionably their best position, that of unusual and *unanticipated* intervals.

On account of the stupidity of some people, or (if talent be a more respectable word), on account of their talent for misconception—I think it necessary to add here, first, that I believe the "processes" above detailed to be nearly if not accurately those which *did* occur in the gradual creation of what we now call verse; secondly, that, although I so believe, I yet urge neither the assumed fact nor my belief in it, as a part of the true propositions of this paper; thirdly, that in regard to the aim of this paper, it is of no consequence whether these processes did occur either in the order I have assigned them, or at all; my design being simply, in presenting a general type of what such processes *might* have been, and *must* have resembled, to help *them,* the "some people," to an easy understanding of what I have farther to say on the topic of Verse.

There is one point which, in my summary of the processes, I have purposely forborne to touch; because this point, being the most important of all, on account of the immensity of error usually involved in its consideration, would have led me into a series of detail inconsistent with the object of a summary.

Every reader of verse must have observed how seldom it happens that even any one line proceeds uniformly with a succession, such as I have supposed, of absolutely equal feet; that is to say, with a succession of iambuses only, or of trochees only, or of dactyls only, or of anapaests only, or of spondees only. Even in the most musical lines we find the succession interrupted. The iambic pentameters of Pope, for example, will be found, on examination, frequently varied by trochees in the beginning, or by (what seem to be) anapaests in the body, of the line.

> Oh *thou* | whate | ver *ti* | tle *please* | thine *ear* |
> Dean *Dra* | pier *Bick* | erstaff | or *Gul* | iver |
> *Whe*ther | thou *choose* | Cervan | tes' *se* | rious *air* |
> Or *laugh* | and *shake* | in *Rab* | elais' *ea* | sy *chair*. |

Were any one weak enough to refer to the prosodies for the solution of the difficulty here, he would find it *solved* as usual by a *rule*, stating the fact (or what it, the rule, supposes to be the fact), but without the slightest attempt at the *rationale*. "By a *synaeresis* of the two short syllables," say the books, "an anapaest may sometimes be employed for an iambus, or a dactyl for a trochee. . . . In the beginning of a line a trochee is often used for an iambus."

Blending is the plain English for *synaeresis*—but there should be *no* blending; neither is an anapaest *ever* employed for an iambus, or a dactyl for a trochee. These feet differ in time; and *no* feet so differing can ever be legitimately used in the same line. An anapaest is equal to four short syllables—an iambus only to three. Dactyls and trochees hold the same relation. The principle of *equality*, in verse, admits, it is true, of variation at certain points, for the relief of monotone, as I have already shown, but the point of *time* is that point which, being the rudimental one, must never be tampered with at all.

To explain:—In farther efforts for the relief of monotone than those to which I have alluded in the summary, men soon came to see that there was no absolute necessity for adhering to the precise number of syllables, provided the time required for the whole foot was preserved inviolate. They saw, for instance, that in such a line as

> Or *laugh* | and *shake* | in *Rab* | elais' *ea* | sy *chair*, |

the equalization of the three syllables *elais' ea* with the two syllables composing any of the other feet, could be readily effected by pronouncing the two syllables *elais'* in double quick time. By pronouncing each of the syllables *e* and *lais'* twice as rapidly as the syllable *sy*, or the syllable *in*, or any other syllable, they could bring the two of them, taken together, to the length, that is to say, to the time, of any one short syllable. This consideration enabled them to affect the agreeable variation of three syllables in place of the uniform two. And variation was the object—variation to the ear. What sense is there, then, in supposing this object rendered null by the *blending* of the two syllables so as to render them, in absolute effect, one? Of course, there must be *no* blending. Each syllable must be pronounced as distinctly as possible (or the variation is lost), but with twice the rapidity in which the ordinary syllable is enunciated. That the syllables *elais' ea* do not compose an *anapaest* is evident, and the signs (a a *a*) of their accentuation are erroneous. The foot might be called a bastard iambus.

Here is a trochaic line:

See the | *deli*cate | *footed* | *rein*-deer. |

The prosodies—that is to say, the most considerate of them—would here decide that "*delicate*" is a dactyl used in place of a trochee, and would refer to what they call their "rule," for justification. Others, varying the stupidity, would insist upon a Procrustean adjustment thus (del'cate)—an adjustment recommended to all such words as *silvery, murmuring*, &c., which, it is said, should be not only pronounced, but written *silv'ry, murm'ring*, and so on, whenever they find themselves in trochaic predicament. I have only to say that "delicate," when circumstanced as above, is neither a dactyl nor a dactyl's equivalent; that I think it as well to call it a bastard trochee; and that all words, at all events, should be written and pronounced *in full*, and as nearly as possible as nature intended them.

About eleven years ago, there appeared in the *American Monthly Magazine* (then edited, I believe, by Messrs. Hoffman and Benjamin) a review of Mr. Willis' Poems; the critic putting forth his strength or his weakness, in an endeavor to show that the poet was either absurdly affected, or grossly ignorant of the laws of verse; the accusation being based altogether on the fact that Mr. W. made occasional use of this very word "delicate," and other similar words, in "the Heroic measure, which every one knew consisted of feet of two syllables." Mr. W. has often, for example, such lines as

That binds him to a woman's *delicate* love—
In the gay sunshine, *reverent* in the storm—
With its *invisible* fingers my loose hair.

Here, of course, the feet *licate love, verent in*, and *sible fin*, are bastard iambuses; are *not* anapaests; and are *not* improperly used. Their employment, on the contrary, by Mr. Willis, is but one of the innumerable instances he has given of keen sensibility in all those matters of taste which may be classed under the general head of *fanciful embellishment*.

It is also about eleven years ago, if I am not mistaken, since Mr. Horne (of England), the author of "Orion," one of the noblest epics in any language, thought it necessary to preface his "Chaucer Modernized" by a very long and evidently a very elaborate essay, of which the greater portion was occupied in a discussion of the seemingly anomalous foot of which we have been speaking. Mr. Horne upholds Chaucer in its frequent use; maintains his superiority, *on account* of his so frequently using it, over all English versifiers; and, indignantly repelling the common idea of those who make verse on their fingers, that the superfluous syllable is a roughness and an error, very chivalrously makes battle for it as "a grace." That a grace it *is*, there can be no doubt; and what I complain of is, that the author of the most happily versified long poem in existence, should have been under the necessity of discussing this grace merely *as* a grace, through forty or fifty vague pages, solely because of his inability to show *how* and *why* it is a grace—by which showing the question would have been settled in an instant.

About the trochee used for an iambus, as we see in the beginning of the line,

> *Whe*ther thou choose Cervantes' serious air,

there is little that need be said. It brings me to the general proposition that in all rhythms, the prevalent or distinctive feet may be varied at will, and nearly at random, by the *occasional* introduction of equivalent feet—that is to say, feet the sum of whose syllabic times is equal to the sum of the syllabic times of the distinctive feet. Thus the trochee *whether*, is equal in the sum of the times of its syllables, to the iambus, *thou choose*, in the sum of the times of *its* syllables; each foot being, in time, equal to three short syllables. Good versifiers, who happen to be, also, good poets, contrive to relieve the monotone of a series of feet, by the use of equivalent feet only at rare intervals, and at such points of their subject as seem in accordance with the *startling* character of the variation. Nothing of this care is seen in the line quoted above—although Pope has some fine instances of the duplicate effect. Where vehemence is to be strongly expressed, I am not sure that we should be wrong in venturing on *two consecutive* equivalent feet— although I cannot say that I have ever known the adventure made, except in the following passage, which occurs in "Al Aaraaf," a boyish poem, written by myself when a boy. I am referring to the sudden and rapid advent of a star:

162

Dim was its little disk, and angel eyes
Alone could see the phantom in the skies,
When first the phantom's course was found to be
*Head*long *hith*erward o'er the starry sea.

In the "general proposition" above, I speak of the *occasional* introduction of equivalent feet. It sometimes happens that unskilful versifiers, without knowing what they do, or why they do it, introduce so
many "variations" as to exceed in number the "distinctive" feet; when
the ear becomes at once balked by the *bouleversement* of the rhythm.
Too many trochees, for example, inserted in an iambic rhythm, would
convert the latter to a trochaic. I may note here, that, in all cases, the
rhythm designed should be commenced and continued, *without* variation, until the ear has had full time to comprehend what *is* the rhythm.
In violation of a rule so obviously founded in common-sense, many
even of our best poets, do not scruple to begin an iambic rhythm with
a trochee, or the converse; or a dactylic with an anapaest, or the converse; and so on.

A somewhat less objectionable error, although still a decided one,
is that of commencing a rhythm, not with a different equivalent foot,
but with a "bastard" foot of the rhythm intended. For example:

*Man*y a | *thought* will | *come* to | *mem*ory. |

Here *many a* is what I have explained to be a bastard trochee, and
to be understood should be accented with inverted crescents. It is
objectionable solely on account of its position as the *opening* foot of a
trochaic rhythm. *Memory*, similarly accented, is also a bastard
trochee, but *un*objectionable, although by no means demanded.

The farther illustration of this point will enable me to take an
important step.

One of the finest poets, Mr. Christopher Pease Cranch, begins a
very beautiful poem thus:

Many are the thoughts that come to me
In my lonely musing;
And they drift so strange and swift
There's no time for choosing
Which to follow; for to leave
Any, seems a losing.

"A losing" to Mr. Cranch, of course—but this *en passant*. It will be
seen here that the intention is trochaic, although we do *not* see this
intention by the opening foot, as we should do—or even by the opening line. Reading the whole stanza, however, we perceive the trochaic
rhythm as the general design, and so, after some reflection, we divide
the first line thus:

163

Many are the | *thoughts* that | *come* to *me*. |

Thus scanned, the line will seem musical. It *is*—highly so. And it is because there is no end to instances of just such lines of apparently incomprehensible music, that Coleridge thought proper to invent his nonsensical *system* of what he calls "scanning by accents"—as if "scanning by accents" were anything more than a phrase. Wherever "Christabel" is really *not rough*, it can be as readily scanned by the true *laws* (not the supposititious *rules*) of verse as can the simplest pentameter of Pope; and where it *is* rough (*passim*), these same laws will enable any one of common-sense to show *why* it is rough, and to point out, instantaneously, the remedy for the roughness.

A reads and re-reads a certain line, and pronounces it false in rhythm—unmusical. *B*, however, reads it *to A*, and *A* is at once struck with the perfection of the rhythm, and wonders at his dullness in not "catching" it before. Henceforward he admits the line to be musical. *B*, triumphant, asserts that, to be sure, the line is musical—for it is the work of Coleridge,—and that it is *A* who is *not;* the fault being in *A's* false reading. Now here *A* is right and *B* wrong. *That* rhythm is erroneous (at some point or other more or less obvious) which *any* ordinary reader *can*, without design, read improperly. It is the business of the poet so to construct his line that the intention *must* be caught *at once*. Even when these men have precisely the same understanding of a sentence, they differ, and often widely, in their modes of enunciating it. Any one who has taken the trouble to examine the topic of emphasis (by which I here mean not *accent* of particular syllables, but the dwelling on entire words), must have seen that men emphasize in the most singularly arbitrary manner. There are certain large classes of people, for example, who persist in emphasizing their monosyllables. Little uniformity of emphasis prevails; because the thing itself—the idea, emphasis—is referable to no natural, at least to no well-comprehended, and therefore uniform, law. Beyond a very narrow and vague limit the whole matter is conventionality. And if we differ in emphasis even when we agree in comprehension, how much more so in the former when in the latter too! Apart, however, from the consideration of natural disagreement, is it not clear that, by tripping here and mouthing there, any sequence of words may be twisted into any species of rhythm? But are we thence to deduce that all sequences of words are rhythmical in a rational understanding of the term?—for this is the deduction, precisely, to which the *reductio ad absurdum* will, in the end, bring all the propositions of Coleridge. Out of a hundred readers of "Christabel," fifty will be able to make nothing of its rhythm, while forty-nine of the remaining fifty will, with some ado, fancy they comprehend it, after the fourth or fifth perusal. The one out of the whole hundred who shall both comprehend and admire it at first sight must be an unaccountably clever person—and I am by far too modest to assume, for a moment, that that very clever person is myself.

In illustration of what is here advanced I cannot do better than quote a poem:

> Pease porridge hot—pease porridge cold—
> Pease porridge in the pot—nine days old.

Now those of my readers who have never *heard* this poem pronounced according to the nursery conventionality, will find its rhythm as obscure as an explanatory note; while those who *have* heard it, will divide it thus, declare it musical, and wonder how there can be any doubt about it.

> Pease | porridge | hot | pease | porridge | cold |
> Pease | porridge | in the | pot | nine | days | old. |

The chief thing in the way of this species of rhythm, is the necessity which it imposes upon the poet of traveling in constant company with his compositions, so as to be ready, at a moment's notice, to avail himself of a well-understood poetical license—that of reading aloud one's own doggerel.

In Mr. Cranch's line,

> Many are the | thoughts that | come to | me, |

the general error of which I speak is, of course, very partially exemplified, and the purpose for which, chiefly, I cite it, lies yet farther on in our topic.

The two divisions, *"thoughts that"* and *"come to,"* are ordinary trochees. Of the last division, *"me,"* we will talk hereafter. The first division, *"many are the,"* would be thus accented by the Greek Prosodies, "many are the," and would be called by them ἀστρολόγος. The Latin books would style the foot *Paeon Primus*, and both Greek and Latin would swear that it was composed of a trochee and what they term a pyrrhic—that is to say, a foot of two *short* syllables—a thing that *cannot be*, as I shall presently show.

But now, there is an obvious difficulty. The *astrologos*, according to the Prosodies' own showing, is equal to *five* short syllables, and the trochee to *three*—yet, in the line quoted, these two feet are equal. They occupy *precisely* the same time. In fact, the whole music of the line depends upon their being *made* to occupy the same time. The Prosodies then, have demonstrated what all mathematicians have stupidly failed in demonstrating—that three and five are one and the same thing.

165

After what I have already said, however, about the bastard trochee and the bastard iambus, no one can have any trouble in understanding that *many are the* is of similar character. It is merely a bolder variation than usual from the routine of trochees, and introduces to the bastard trochee one additional syllable. But this syllable is not *short*. That is, it is not short in the sense of *"short"* as applied to the final syllable of the ordinary trochee, where the word means merely *the half of long*.

In this case (that of the additional syllable), "short," if used at all, must be used in the sense of *the sixth of long*. And all the three final syllables can be called *short* only with the same understanding of the term. The three together are equal only to the one short syllable (whose place they supply) of the ordinary trochee. It follows that there is no sense in thus (ᵕ) accenting these syllables. We must devise for them some new character which shall denote the sixth of long. Let it be (( )—the crescent placed with the curve to the left. The whole foot (many are the) might be called a *quick trochee*.

We come now to the final division, *"me,"* of Mr. Cranch's line. It is clear that this foot, short as it appears, is fully equal in time to each of the preceding. It is in fact the caesura—the foot which, in the beginning of this paper, I called the most important in all verse. Its chief office is that of pause or termination; and here—at the end of a line—its use is easy, because there is no danger of misapprehending its value. We pause on it, by a seeming necessity, just as long as it has taken us to pronounce the preceding feet, whether iambuses, trochees, dactyls, or anapaests. It is thus a *variable foot*, and, with some care, may be well introduced into the body of a line, as in a little poem of great beauty by Mrs. Welby:

I have | a lit | tle step | son | of on | ly three | years old. |

Here we dwell on the caesura, *son*, just as long as it requires us to pronounce either of the preceding or succeeding iambuses. Its value, therefore, in this line, is that of three short syllables. In the following dactylic line its value is that of four short syllables.

Pale as a | lily was | Emily | Gray.

I have accented the caesura with a dotted line (⋯⋯) by way of expressing this variability of value.

I observed just now that there could be no such foot as one of two short syllables. What we start from in the very beginning of all idea on the topic of verse, is quantity, *length*. Thus when we enunciate an independent syllable it is long, as a matter of course. If we enunciate two, dwelling on both equally, we express equality in the enumeration, or length, and have a right to call them two long syllables. If we dwell on one more than the other, we have also a right to call one short, because it is short in relation to the other. But if we dwell on both equally and with a tripping voice, saying to ourselves here are two short syllables, the query might well be asked of us—"in relation to what are they short?" Shortness is but the negation of length. To say, then, that two syllables, placed independently of any other syllable, are short, is merely to say that they have no positive length, or enunciation—in other words that they are not syllables—that they do not exist at all. And if, persisting, we add anything about their equality, we are merely floundering in the idea of an identical equation, where, x being equal to x, nothing is shown to be equal to zero. In a word, we can form no conception of a pyrrhic as of an independent foot. It is a mere chimera bred in the mad fancy of a pedant.

From what I have said about the equalization of the several feet of a *line*, it must not be deduced that any *necessity* for equality in time exists between the rhythm of *several* lines. A poem, or even a stanza, may begin with iambuses, in the first line, and proceed with anapaests in the second, or even with the less accordant dactyls, as in the opening of quite a pretty specimen of verse by Miss Mary A. S. Aldrich.

> The wa | ter li | ly sleeps | in pride |
>
> *Down* in the | *depths* of the | *azure* | lake. |

Here *azure* is a spondee, equivalent to a dactyl; *lake*, a caesura.

I shall now best proceed in quoting the initial lines of Byron's "Bride of Abydos":

> Know ye the land where the cypress and myrtle
> Are emblems of deeds that are done in their clime—
> Where the rage of the vulture, the love of the turtle
> Now melt into softness, now madden to crime?
> Know ye the land of the cedar and vine,
> Where the flowers ever blossom, the beams ever shine,
> And the light wings of Zephyr, oppressed with perfume,
> Wax faint o'er the gardens of Gul in their bloom?
> Where the citron and olive are fairest of fruit
> And the voice of the nightingale never is mute;
>
> . . . . . .
>
> Where the virgins are soft as the roses they twine,
> And all save the spirit of man is divine?
> 'Tis the land of the East—'tis the clime of the Sun—
> Can he smile on such deeds as his children have done?
> Oh, wild as the accents of lovers' farewell
> Are the hearts that they bear and the tales that they tell!

167

Now the flow of these lines (as times go) is very sweet and musical. They have been often admired, and justly—as times go,—that is to say, it is a rare thing to find better versification of its kind. And where verse is pleasant to the ear, it is silly to find fault with it because it refuses to be scanned. Yet I have heard men, professing to be scholars, who made no scruple of abusing these lines of Byron's on the ground that they were musical in spite of *all law*. Other gentlemen, *not* scholars, abused "all law" for the same reason; and it occurred neither to the one party nor to the other that the law about which they were disputing might possibly be no law at all—an ass of a law in the skin of a lion.

The grammars said something about dactylic lines, and it was easily seen that *these* lines were at least meant for dactylic. The first one was, therefore, thus divided:

Know ye the | *land* where the | *cy*press and | *myr*tle. |

The concluding foot was a mystery; but the Prosodies said something about the dactylic "measure" calling now and then for a double rhyme; and the court of inquiry were content to rest in the double rhyme, without exactly perceiving what a double rhyme had to do with the question of an irregular foot. Quitting the first line, the second was thus scanned:

Are emblems | *of* deeds that | *are* done in | their clime. |

It was immediately seen, however, that *this* would not do,—it was at war with the whole emphasis of the reading. It could not be supposed that Byron, or any one in his senses, intended to place stress upon such monosyllables as "are," "of," and "their," nor could "their clime," collated with "to crime," in the corresponding line below, be fairly twisted into anything like a "double rhyme," so as to bring everything within the category of the grammars. But farther these grammars spoke not. The inquirers, therefore, in spite of their sense of harmony in the lines, when considered without reference to scansion, fell back upon the idea that the "Are" was a blunder,—an excess for which the poet should be sent to Coventry,—and, striking it out, they scanned the remainder of the line as follows:

—*em*blems of | *deeds* that are | *done* in their | *clime*. |

This answered pretty well; but the grammars admitted no such foot as a foot of one syllable; and besides the rhythm was dactylic. In despair, the books are well searched, however, and at last the investigators are gratified by a full solution of the riddle in the profound "Observation" quoted in the beginning of this article:—"When a syllable is wanting, the verse is said to be catalectic; when the measure is exact, the line is acatalectic; when there is a redundant syllable it forms hypermeter." This is enough. The anomalous line is pronounced to be catalectic at the head and to form hypermeter at the tail,—and so on, and so on; it being soon discovered that nearly all the remaining lines are in a similar predicament, and that what flows so smoothly to the ear, although so roughly to the eye, is, after all, a mere jumble of catalecticism, acatalecticism, and hypermeter—not to say worse.

Now, had this court of inquiry been in possession of even the shadow of the *philosophy* of verse, they would have had no trouble in reconciling this oil and water of the eye and ear, by merely scanning the passage without reference to lines, and, continuously, thus:

Know ye the | land where the | cypress and | myrtle Are | emblems of | deeds that are | done in their | clime Where the | rage of the | vulture the | love of the | turtle Now | melt into | softness now | madden to | *crime* | Know ye the | land of the | cedar and | vine Where the | flowers ever | blossom the | beams ever | shine Where the | light wings of | Zephyr op | pressed with per | *fume Wax* | faint o'er the | gardens of | Gul in their | bloom Where the | citron and | olive are | fairest of | fruit And the | voice of the | nightingale | never is | mute Where the | virgins are | soft as the | roses they | *twine And* | all save the | spirit of | man is di | vine 'Tis the | land of the | East 'tis the | clime of the | Sun Can he | smile on such | deeds as his | children have | *done Oh* | wild as the | accents of | lovers' fare | well Are the | hearts that they | bear and the | tales that they | *tell.*

Here "crime" and "tell" (italicized) are caesuras, each having the value of a dactyl, four short syllables; while "*fume Wax*," "*twine And*," and "*done Oh*," are spondees, which, of course, being composed of two long syllables, are also equal to four short, and are the dactyl's natural equivalent. The nicety of Byron's ear has led him into a succession of feet which, with two trivial exceptions as regards melody, are absolutely accurate—a very rare occurrence this in dactylic or anapaestic rhythms. The exceptions are found in the spondee "*twine And*," and the dactyl, "*smile on such*." Both feet are false in point of melody. In "*twine And*," to make out the rhythm, we must force "*And*" into a length which it will not naturally bear. We are called on to sacrifice either the proper length of the syllable as demanded by its position as a member of a spondee, or the customary accentuation of the word in conversation. There is no hesitation, and should be none. We at once give up the sound for the sense; and the rhythm is imperfect. In this instance it is *very* slightly so;—not one person in ten thousand could, by ear, detect the inaccuracy. But the *perfection* of verse, as regards melody, consists in its *never* demanding any such sacrifice as is here demanded. The rhythmical must agree, *thoroughly*, with the reading flow. This perfection has in no instance been attained—but is unquestionably attainable. *"Smile on such,"* the dactyl, is incorrect, because *"such,"* from the character of the two consonants *ch,* cannot *easily* be enunciated in the ordinary time of a short syllable, which its position declares that it is. Almost every reader will be able to appreciate the slight difficulty here; and yet the error is by no means so important as that of the *"And"* in the spondee. By dexterity we *may* pronounce *"such"* in the true time; but the attempt to remedy the rhythmical deficiency of the *"And"* by drawing it out, merely aggravates the offence against natural enunciation, by directing attention to the offence.

My main object, however, in quoting these lines, is to show that, in spite of the Prosodies, the length of a line is entirely an arbitrary matter. We might divide the commencement of Byron's poem thus:

Know ye the | land where the |

or thus:

Know ye the | land where the | cypress and |

or thus:

Know ye the | land where the | cypress and | myrtle are |

or thus:

Know ye the | land where the | cypress and | myrtle are | emblems of |

In short, we may give it any division we please, and the lines will be good—provided we have at least *two* feet in a line. As in mathematics two units are required to form number, so rhythm (from the Greek ἀριθμός, number) demands for its formation at least two feet. Beyond doubt, we often see such lines as

Know ye the—
Land where the—

lines of one foot; and our Prosodies admit such; but with impropriety: for common-sense would dictate that every so obvious division of a poem as is made by a line, should include within itself all that is necessary for its own comprehension; but in a line of one foot we can have no appreciation of *rhythm,* which depends upon the equality between *two* or more pulsations. The false lines, consisting sometimes of a single caesura, which are seen in mock Pindaric odes, are of course "rhythmical" only in connection with some other line; and it is this want of independent rhythm which adapts them to the purposes of

170

burlesque alone. Their effect is that of incongruity (the principle of mirth), for they include the blankness of prose amid the harmony of verse.

My second object in quoting Byron's lines, was that of showing how absurd it often is to cite a single line from amid the body of a poem, for the purpose of instancing the perfection or imperfection of the line's rhythm. Were we to see by itself

Know ye the land where the cypress and myrtle,

we might justly condemn it as defective in the final foot, which is equal to only three, instead of being equal to four, short syllables.

In the foot "*flowers ever*" we shall find a further exemplification of the principle of the bastard iambus, bastard trochee, and quick trochee, as I have been at some pains in describing these feet above. All the Prosodies on English verse would insist upon making an elision in "*flowers*," thus "*flow'rs*," but this is nonsense. In the quick trochee "*many are the*" occurring in Mr. Cranch's *trochaic* line, we had to equalize the time of the three syllables "*any, are, the*" to that of the one *short* syllable whose position they usurp. Accordingly each of these syllables is equal to the third of a short syllable—that is to say, the *sixth of a long*. But in Byron's *dactylic* rhythm, we have to equalize the time of the three syllables "*ers, ev, er*" to that of the one *long* syllable whose position they usurp, or (which is the same thing) of the *two short*. Therefore, the value of each of the syllables "*ers, ev,* and *er*" is the *third of a long*. We enunciate them with only half the rapidity we employ in enunciating the three final syllables of the quick trochee—which latter is a rare foot. The "*flowers ever*," on the contrary, is as common in the dactylic rhythm as is the *bastard* trochee in the trochaic, or the bastard iambus in the iambic. We may as well accent it with the curve of the crescent to the right, and call it a *bastard dactyl*. A *bastard anapaest*, whose nature I now need be at no trouble in explaining, will of course occur, now and then, in an anapaestic rhythm.

In order to avoid any chance of that confusion which is apt to be introduced in an essay of this kind by too sudden and radical an alteration of the conventionalities to which the reader has been accustomed, I have thought it right to suggest for the accent marks of the bastard trochee, bastard iambus, &c., &c., certain characters which, in merely varying the direction of the ordinary short accent (ᴗ), should imply, what is the fact, that the feet themselves are not *new* feet, in any proper sense, but simply modifications of the feet, respectively, from which they derive their names. Thus a bastard iambus is, in its essentiality,—that is to say, in its time,—an iambus. The variation lies only in the *distribution* of this time. The time, for example, occupied by the one short (or *half of long*) syllable, in the ordinary iambus, is, in the bastard, spread equally over two syllables, which are accordingly the *fourth of long*.

But this fact—the fact of the essentiality, or whole time, of the foot being unchanged—is now so fully before the reader that I may venture to propose, finally, an accentuation which shall answer the real purpose—that is to say, what should be the real purpose—of all accentuation: the purpose of expressing to the eye the exact relative value of every syllable employed in Verse.

I have already shown that enunciation, or *length*, is the point from which we start. In other words, we begin with a *long syllable*. This, then, is our unit; and there will be no need of accenting it at all. An unaccented syllable, in a system of accentuation, is to be regarded always as a long syllable. Thus a spondee would be without accent. In an iambus, the first syllable being "short," or the *half* of long, should be accented with a small 2, placed *beneath* the syllable; the last syllable, being long, should be unaccented: the whole would be thus (control). In a trochee, these accents would be merely conversed, thus (mǎnly). In a dactyl, each of the two final syllables, being the half of long, should, also, be accented with a small 2 beneath the syllable; and, the first syllable left unaccented, the whole would be thus (happiness). In an anapaest we should converse the dactyl, thus (in the land). In the bastard dactyl, each of the three concluding syllables being the *third* of long, should be accented with a small 3 beneath the syllable, and the whole foot would stand thus (flowers ever). In the bastard anapaest we should converse the bastard dactyl, thus (in the rebound). In the bastard iambus, each of the two initial syllables, being the *fourth* of long, should be accented below with a small 4; the whole foot would be thus (in the rain). In the bastard trochee we should converse the bastard iambus, thus (many a). In the quick trochee, each of the three concluding syllables, being the *sixth* of long, should be accented below with a small 6; the whole foot would be thus (many are the). The quick iambus is not yet created, and most probably never will be, for it will be excessively useless, awkward, and liable to misconception,—as I have already shown that even the quick trochee is, —but, should it appear, we must accent it by conversing the quick trochee. The caesura, being variable in length, but always *longer than* "*long*," should be accented *above*, with a number expressing the length or value of the distinctive foot of the rhythm in which it occurs. Thus

172

a caesura, occurring in a spondaic rhythm, would be accented with a small 2 above the syllable, or, rather, foot. Occurring in a dactylic or anapaestic rhythm, we also accent it with the 2, above the foot. Occurring in an iambic rhythm, however, it must be accented, above, with $1\frac{1}{2}$, for this is the relative value of the iambus. Occurring in the trochaic rhythm, we give it, of course, the same accentuation. For the complex $1\frac{1}{2}$, however, it would be advisable to substitute the simpler expression, $\frac{3}{2}$, which amounts to the same thing.

In this system of accentuation Mr. Cranch's lines, quoted above, would thus be written:

$$\frac{3}{2}$$

Many are the | thoughts that | come to | me
　　6　　6　　6　　　　　　2　　　2
In my | lonely | musing, |
　　2　　　2　　　　2

$$\frac{3}{2}$$

And they | drift so | strange and | swift
　　2　　　2　　　　　　2
There's no time for | choosing |
　　　2　　　　2　　　　2

$$\frac{3}{2}$$

Which to | follow, | for to | leave
　　2　　　2　　　2
Any | seems a | losing. |
　2　　　　2

In the ordinary system the accentuation would be thus:

Many are the | *thoughts* that | *come* to | me
In my | *lone*ly | *mus*ing. |
And they | *drift* so | *strange* and | *swift* |
There 's no | *time* for | *choos*ing |
Which to | *fol*low, | *for* to | leave
Any | *seems* a | *los*ing. |

It must be observed here that I do not grant this to be the "ordinary" *scansion*. On the contrary, I never yet met the man who had the faintest comprehension of the true scanning of these lines, or of such as these. But granting this to be the mode in which our Prosodies would divide the feet, they would accentuate the syllables as just above.

Now, let any reasonable person compare the two modes. The first advantage seen in my mode is that of simplicity—of time, labor, and ink saved. Counting the fractions as *two* accents, even, there will be found only *twenty-six* accents to the stanza. In the common accentuation there are *forty-one*. But admit that all this is a trifle, which it is

173

not, and let us proceed to points of importance. Does the common accentuation express the truth in particular, in general, or in any regard? Is it consistent with itself? Does it convey either to the ignorant or to the scholar a just conception of the rhythm of the lines? Each of these questions must be answered in the negative. The crescents, being precisely similar, must be understood as expressing, all of them, one and the same thing; and so all Prosodies have always understood them and wished them to be understood. They express, indeed, "short"; but this word has all kinds of meanings. It serves to represent (the reader is left to guess *when*) sometimes the half, sometimes the third, sometimes the fourth, sometimes the sixth of "long"; while "long" itself, in the books, is left undefined and undescribed. On the other hand, the horizontal accent, it may be said, expresses sufficiently well and unvaryingly the syllables which are meant to be long. It does nothing of the kind. This horizontal accent is placed over the caesura (wherever, as in the Latin Prosodies, the caesura is recognized) as well as over the ordinary long syllable, and implies anything and everything, just as the crescent. But grant that it does express the ordinary long syllables (leaving the caesura out of question), have I not given the identical expression by not employing any expression at all? In a word, while the Prosodies, with a certain number of accents express *precisely nothing whatever,* I, with scarcely half the number, have expressed everything which, in a system of accentuation, demands expression. In glancing at my mode in the lines of Mr. Cranch it will be seen that it conveys not only the exact relation of the syllables and feet, among themselves, in those particular lines, but their precise value in relation to any other existing or conceivable feet or syllables in any existing or conceivable system of rhythm.

The object of what we call *scansion* is the distinct marking of the rhythmical flow. Scansion with accents or perpendicular lines between the feet—that is to say, scansion *by* the voice only—is scansion *to* the ear only; and all very good in its way. The written scansion addresses the ear through the eye. In either case the object is the distinct marking of the rhythmical, musical, or reading flow. There *can* be no other object, and there is none. Of course, then, the scansion and the reading flow should go hand-in-hand. The former must agree with the latter. The former represents and expresses the latter; and is good or bad as it truly or falsely represents and expresses it. If by the written scansion of a line we are not enabled to perceive any rhythm or music in the line, then either the line is unrhythmical or the scansion false. Apply all this to the English lines which we have quoted, at various points, in the course of this article. It will be found that the scansion exactly conveys the rhythm, and thus thoroughly fulfils the only purpose for which scansion is required.

But let the scansion *of the schools* be applied to the Greek and Latin verse, and what result do we find?—that the verse is one thing and the scansion quite another. The ancient verse, *read* aloud, is in general musical, and occasionally *very* musical. *Scanned* by the prosodial rules we can, for the most part, make nothing of it whatever. In the case of the English verse, the more emphatically we dwell on the divisions between the feet, the more distinct is our perception of the kind of rhythm intended. In the case of the Greek and Latin, the more we dwell the *less* distinct is this perception. To make this clear by an example:

> Maecenas, atavis edite regibus,
> O, et praesidium et dulce decus meum,
> Sunt quos curriculo pulverem Olympicum
> Collegisse juvat, metaque fervidis
> Evitata rotis, palmaque nobilis
> Terrarum dominos evehit ad Deos.

Now in *reading* these lines, there is scarcely one person in a thousand who, if even ignorant of Latin, will not immediately feel and appreciate their flow—their music. A prosodist, however, informs the public that the *scansion* runs thus:

> Maece | nas ata | vis | edite | regibus |
> O et | praesidi' | et | dulce de | cus meum |
> Sunt quos | curricu | lo | pulver' O | lympicum
> Colle | gisse ju | vat | metaque | fervidis |
> Evi | tata ro | tis | palmaque | nobilis |
> Terra | rum domi | nos | evehit | ad Deos. |

Now I do not deny that we get a *certain sort* of music from the lines if we read them according to this scansion, but I wish to call attention to the fact that this scansion, and the certain sort of music which grows out of it, are entirely at war not only with the reading flow which any ordinary person would naturally give the lines, but with the reading flow universally given them, and never denied them, by even the most obstinate and stolid of scholars.

And now these questions are forced upon us: "Why exists this discrepancy between the modern verse with its scansion, and the ancient verse with its scansion?"—"Why, in the former case, are there agreement and representation, while in the latter there is neither the one nor the other?" or, to come to the point,—"How are we to reconcile the ancient verse with the scholastic scansion of it?" This absolutely necessary conciliation—shall we bring it about by supposing the scholastic scansion wrong because the ancient verse is right, or by maintaining that the ancient verse is wrong because the scholastic scansion is not to be gainsaid?

Were we to adopt the latter mode of arranging the difficulty, we might, in some measure, at least simplify the expression of the arrangement by putting it thus: Because the pedants have no eyes, therefore the old poets had no ears.

"But," say the gentlemen without the eyes, "the scholastic scansion, although certainly not handed down to us in form from the old poets themselves (the gentlemen without the ears), is nevertheless deduced from certain facts which are supplied us by careful observation of the old poems."

And let us illustrate this strong position by an example from an American poet—who must be a poet of some eminence, or he will not answer the purpose. Let us take Mr. Alfred B. Street. I remember these two lines of his:

> His sinuous path, by blazes, wound
> Among trunks grouped in myriads round.

With the *sense* of these lines I have nothing to do. When a poet is in a "fine frenzy," he may as well imagine a large forest as a small one; and "by blazes" is *not* intended for an oath. My concern is with the rhythm, which is iambic.

Now let us suppose that, a thousand years hence, when the "American language" is dead, a learned prosodist should be deducing, from "careful observation" of our best poets, a system of scansion for our poetry. And let us suppose that this prosodist had so little dependence in the generality and immutability of the laws of Nature, as to assume in the outset, that, because we lived a thousand years before his time, and made use of steam-engines instead of mesmeric balloons, we must therefore have had a *very* singular fashion of mouthing our vowels, and altogether of Hudsonizing our verse. And let us suppose that with these and other fundamental propositions carefully put away in his brain, he should arrive at the line,—

> Among | trunks grouped | in my | riads round.

Finding it an obviously iambic rhythm, he would divide it as above; and observing that "trunks" made the first member of an iambus, he would call it short, as Mr. Street intended it to be. Now farther, if instead of admitting the possibility that Mr. Street (who by that time would be called Street simply, just as we say Homer)—that Mr. Street might have been in the habit of writing carelessly, as the poets of the prosodist's own era did, and as all poets will do (on account of being geniuses),—instead of admitting this, suppose the learned scholar should make a "rule" and put it in a book, to the effect that, in the American verse, the vowel *u*, *when found imbedded among nine consonants*, was *short*, what, under such circumstances, would the sensible people of the scholar's day have a right not only to think but to say of that scholar?—why, that he was "a fool—by blazes!"

I have put an extreme case, but it strikes at the root of the error. The "rules" are grounded in "authority"; and this "authority"—can any one tell us what it means? or can any one suggest anything that it may *not* mean? Is it not clear that the "scholar" above referred to, might as readily have deduced from authority a totally false system as a partially true one? To deduce from authority a consistent prosody of the ancient metres would indeed have been within the limits of the barest possibility; and the task has *not* been accomplished, for the reason that it demands a species of ratiocination altogether out of keeping with the brain of a bookworm. A rigid scrutiny will show that the very few "rules" which have not as many exceptions as examples, are those which have, by accident, their true bases not in authority, but in the omniprevalent laws of syllabification; such, for example, as the rule which declares a vowel before two consonants to be long.

In a word, the gross confusion and antagonism of the scholastic prosody, as well as its marked inapplicability to the reading flow of the rhythms it pretends to illustrate, are attributable, first, to the utter absence of natural principle as a guide in the investigations which have been undertaken by inadequate men; and secondly to the neglect of the obvious consideration that the ancient poems, which have been the *criteria* throughout, were the work of men who must have written as loosely, and with as little definitive system, as ourselves.

Were Horace alive to-day, he would divide for us his first Ode thus, and "make great eyes" when assured by prosodists that he had no business to make any such division:—

$$\text{Maecenas} \mid \underset{2\ \ \ 2}{\text{atavis}} \mid \underset{2\ \ 2}{\text{edite}} \mid \underset{2\ \ 2}{\text{regibus}}$$

$$\underset{2\ \ \ 2}{\text{O et præ}} \mid \underset{3\ \ 3\ \ 3}{\text{sidium et}} \mid \underset{2\ \ \ 2}{\text{dulce de}} \mid \underset{2\ \ 2}{\text{cus meum}} \mid$$

$$\underset{2\ \ \ 2}{\text{Sunt quos cur}} \mid \underset{2\ \ 2}{\text{riculo}} \mid \underset{3\ \ 3\ \ 3}{\text{pulverem O}} \mid \underset{2\ \ 2}{\text{lympicum}} \mid$$

$$\underset{3\ \ 3\ \ 3}{\text{Collegisse}} \mid \underset{2\ \ \ 2}{\text{juvat}} \mid \text{metaque} \mid \underset{2\ \ 2}{\text{fervidis}} \mid$$

$$\underset{3\ \ \ 3\ \ 3}{\text{Evitata}} \mid \underset{2\ \ 2}{\text{rotis}} \mid \text{palmaque} \mid \underset{2\ \ 2}{\text{nobilis}}$$

$$\underset{2\ \ \ 2}{\text{Terrarum}} \mid \underset{2\ \ \ 2}{\text{dominos}} \mid \underset{2\ \ \ 2}{\text{evehit}} \mid \underset{2\ \ 2}{\text{ad Deos.}}$$

Read by this scansion, the flow is preserved; and the more we dwell on the divisions, the more the intended rhythm becomes apparent. Moreover, the feet have all the same time; while, in the scholastic scansion, trochees—admitted trochees—are absurdly employed as equivalents to spondees and dactyls. The books declare, for instance, that *Colle,* which begins the fourth line, is a trochee, and seem to be gloriously unconscious that to put a trochee in opposition with a longer foot, is to violate the inviolable principle of all music, *time.*

It will be said, however, by "some people," that I have no business to make a dactyl out of such obviously long syllables as *sunt, quos, cur.* Certainly I have no business to do so. I *never* do so. And Horace should not have done so. But he did. Mr. Bryant and Mr. Longfellow do the same thing every day. And merely because these gentlemen, now and then, forget themselves in this way, it would be hard if some future prosodist should insist upon twisting the "Thanatopsis," or the "Spanish Student," into a jumble of trochees, spondees, and dactyls.

It may be said, also, by some other people, that in the word *decus,* I have succeeded no better than the books, in making the scansional agree with the reading flow; and that *decus* was not pronounced de*cus.* I reply, that there can be no doubt of the word having been pronounced, in this case, de*cus.* It must be observed, that the Latin inflection, or variation of a word in its terminating syllable, caused the Romans—*must* have caused them—to pay greater attention to the termination of a word than to its commencement, or than we do to the terminations of our words. The end of the Latin word established that relation of the word with other words which we establish by prepositions or auxiliary verbs. Therefore, it would seem infinitely less odd to them than it does to us, to dwell at any time, for any slight purpose, abnormally, on a terminating syllable. In verse, this license—scarcely a license—would be frequently admitted. These ideas unlock the secret of such lines as the

> Litoreis ingens inventa sub ilici*bus sus,*

and the

> Parturiunt montes; nascetur ridicu*lus mus,*

which I quoted, some time ago, while speaking of rhyme.

As regards the prosodial elisions, such as that of *rem* before *O*, in *pulverem Olympicum,* it is really difficult to understand how so dismally silly a notion could have entered the brain even of a pedant. Were it demanded of me why the books cut off one *vowel* before another, I might say: It is, perhaps, because the books think that, since a bad reader is so apt to slide the one vowel into the other at any rate, it is just as well to print them *ready-slided.* But in the case of the terminating *m*, which is the most readily pronounced of all consonants (as the infantile *mamma* will testify), and the most impossible to cheat

178

the ear of by any system of sliding—in the case of the *m*, I should be driven to reply that, to the best of my belief, the prosodists did the thing, because they had a fancy for doing it, and wished to see how funny it would look after it was done. The thinking reader will perceive that, from the great facility with which *em* may be enunciated, it is admirably suited to form one of the rapid short syllables in the bastard dactyl (pulverem O); but because the books had no conception of a bastard dactyl, they knocked it on the head at once—by cutting off its tail!

Let me now give a specimen of the true scansion of another Horatian measure—embodying an instance of proper elision.

$$\text{Integer} \mid \text{vitae} \mid \underset{2\ \ 2}{\text{scelerisque}} \mid \underset{3\ \ 3\ \ 3}{\text{purus}} \mid$$
$$\underset{2\ \ 2}{\text{Non eget}} \mid \text{Mauri} \mid \underset{3\ \ 3\ \ 3}{\text{jaculis ne}} \mid \text{que arcu} \mid$$
$$\underset{2\ \ 2}{\text{Nec vene}} \mid \text{natis} \mid \underset{3\ \ 3\ \ 3}{\text{gravida sa}} \mid \text{gittis} \mid$$
$$\underset{2\ \ \ \ \ \ 2}{\text{Fusce pha}} \mid \text{retrâ.}$$

Here the regular recurrence of the bastard dactyl gives great animation to the rhythm. The *e* before the *a* in *que arcu*, is, almost of sheer necessity, cut off—that is to say, run into the *a* so as to preserve the spondee. But even this license it would have been better not to take.

Had I space, nothing would afford me greater pleasure than to proceed with the scansion of *all* the ancient rhythms, and to show how easily, by the help of common-sense, the intended music of each and all can be rendered instantaneously apparent. But I have already overstepped my limits, and must bring this paper to an end.

It will never do, however, to omit all mention of the heroic hexameter.

I began the "processes" by a suggestion of the spondee as the first step toward verse. But the innate monotony of the spondee has caused its disappearance, as the basis of rhythm, from all modern poetry. We *may* say, indeed, that the French heroic—the most wretchedly monotonous verse in existence—is, to all intents and purposes, spondaic. But it is not designedly spondaic—and if the French were ever to examine it at all, they would no doubt pronounce it iambic. It must be observed that the French language is strangely peculiar in this point —*that it is without accentuation, and consequently without verse.* The genius of the people, rather than the structure of the tongue, declares that their words are, for the most part, enunciated with a uniform dwelling on each syllable. For example, *we* say "syll*a*bifi*ca*tion." A Frenchman would say syl-la-bi-fi-ca-ti-on; dwelling on no one of the syllables with any noticeable particularity. Here again I put an extreme case, in order to be well understood; but the general fact is as I give it—that, comparatively, the French have *no* accentuation. And there can be nothing worth the name of verse without. Therefore, the French have no verse worth the name—which is the fact, put in sufficiently plain terms. Their iambic rhythm so superabounds in absolute spondees, as to warrant me in calling its basis spondaic; but French is the *only* modern tongue which has any rhythm with such basis; and even in the French, it is, as I have said, unintentional.

Admitting, however, the validity of my suggestion, that the spondee was the first approach to verse, we should expect to find, first, natural spondees (words each forming just a spondee) most abundant in the most ancient languages; and, secondly, we should expect to find spondees forming the basis of the most ancient rhythms. These expectations are in both cases confirmed.

Of the Greek hexameter, the intentional basis is spondaic. The dactyls are the *variation* of the theme. It will be observed that there is no absolute certainty about *their* points of interposition. The penultimate foot, it is true, is usually a dactyl; but not uniformly so; while the ultimate, on which the ear *lingers,* is always a spondee. Even that the penultimate is usually a dactyl may be clearly referred to the necessity of winding up with the *distinctive* spondee. In corroboration of this idea, again, we should look to find the penultimate spondee most usual in the most ancient verse; and, accordingly, we find it more frequent in the Greek than in the Latin hexameter.

But besides all this, spondees are not only more prevalent in the heroic hexameter than dactyls, but occur to such an extent as is even unpleasant to modern ears, on account of monotony. What the modern chiefly appreciates and admires in the Greek hexameter, is the *melody of the abundant vowel sounds*. The Latin hexameters *really* please very few moderns—although so many pretend to fall into ecstasies about them. In the hexameters quoted, several pages ago, from Silius Italicus, the preponderance of the spondee is strikingly manifest. Besides the natural spondees of the Greek and Latin, numerous artificial ones arise in the verse of these tongues on account of the tendency which inflection has to throw full accentuation on terminal syllables; and the preponderance of the spondee is farther insured by the comparative infrequency of the small prepositions which *we* have to serve us *instead* of case, and also the absence of the diminutive auxiliary verbs with which *we* have to eke out the expression of our primary ones. These are the monosyllables whose abundance serves to stamp the poetic genius of a language as tripping or dactylic.

Now, paying no attention to these facts, Sir Philip Sidney, Professor Longfellow, and innumerable other persons more or less modern, have busied themselves in constructing what they suppose to be

"English hexameters on the model of the Greek." The only difficulty was that (even leaving out of question the melodious masses of vowels) these gentlemen never could get their English hexameters to *sound* Greek. Did they *look* Greek?—that should have been the query; and the reply might have led to a solution of the riddle. In placing a copy of ancient hexameters side by side with a copy (in similar type) of such hexameters as Professor Longfellow, or Professor Felton, or the Frogpondian Professors collectively, are in the shameful practice of composing "on the model of the Greek," it will be seen that the latter (hexameters, not professors) are about one third longer *to the eye*, on an average, than the former. The more abundant dactyls make the difference. And it is the greater number of spondees in the Greek than in the English—in the ancient than in the modern tongue—which has caused it to fall out that while these eminent scholars were groping about in the dark for a Greek hexameter, which is a spondaic rhythm varied now and then by dactyls, they merely stumbled, to the lasting scandal of scholarship, over something which, on account of its long-leggedness, we may as well term a Feltonian hexameter, and which is a dactylic rhythm, interrupted, rarely, by artificial spondees which are no spondees at all, and which are curiously thrown in by the heels at all kinds of improper and impertinent points.

Here is a specimen of the Longfellownian hexameter.

Also the | church with | in was a | dorned for | this was the | season
In which the | young their | parents' | hope and the | loved ones of |
    Heaven |
Should at the | foot of the | altar re | new the | vows of their | baptism |
Therefore each | nook and | corner was | swept and | cleaned and the |
    dust was |
Blown from the | walls and | ceiling and | from the | oil-painted |
    benches |

Mr. Longfellow is a man of imagination—but *can* he imagine that any individual, with a proper understanding of the danger of lock-jaw, would make the attempt of twisting his mouth into the shape necessary for the emission of such spondees as "par*ents*," and "from the," or such dactyls as "cleaned and the," and "loved ones of"? "Baptism" is by no means a bad spondee—perhaps because it happens to be a dactyl;—of all the rest, however, I am dreadfully ashamed.

But these feet—dactyls and spondees, all together—should thus be put at once into their proper position:

"Also, the church within was adorned; for this was the season in which the young, their parents' hope, and the loved ones of Heaven, should, at the foot of the altar, renew the vows of their baptism. There-fore each nook and corner was swept and cleaned; and the dust was blown from the walls and ceiling, and from the oil-painted benches."

There!—That is respectable prose; and it will incur no danger of ever getting its character ruined by anybody's mistaking it for verse.

But even when we let these modern hexameters go, as Greek, and merely hold them fast in their proper character of Longfellownian, or Feltonian, or Frogpondian, we must still condemn them as having been committed in a radical misconception of the philosophy of verse. The spondee, as I observed, is the *theme* of the Greek line. Most of the ancient hexameters *begin* with spondees, for the reason that the spon-dee *is* the theme; and the ear is filled with it as with a burden. Now the Feltonian dactylics have, in the same way, dactyls for the theme, and most of them begin with dactyls—which is all very proper if not very Greek,—but, unhappily, the one point at which they *are* very Greek is that point, precisely, at which they should be nothing but Feltonian. They always *close* with what is meant for a spondee. To be consistently silly, they should die off in a dactyl.

That a truly Greek hexameter *cannot*, however, be readily com-posed in English, is a proposition which I am by no means inclined to admit. I think I could manage the point myself. For example:

Do tell! | when may we | hope to make | men of sense | out of the |
      Pundits |
Born and brought | up with their | snouts deep | down in the | mud of
      the | Frog-pond? |
Why ask? | who ever | yet saw | money made | out of a | fat old |
Jew, or | downright | upright | nutmegs | out of a | pine-knot? |

The proper spondee predominance is here preserved. Some of the dactyls are not so good as I could wish—but, upon the whole, the rhythm is very decent—to say nothing of its excellent sense.

The Poems of Edgar Allan Poe

VIII

POEMS COLLECTED AFTER 1845

Poe's posthumously collected poems have been variously assigned. Some of them can be identified with certainty. "To my Mother" is a tribute to Poe's aunt, Maria Clemm, who was, in many ways, more than his mother. "To M. L. S——" and "To —— ——" are dedicated to Maria Louise Shew, whose nursing comforted Virginia and probably saved Poe from death. "To Helen" does not refer to Mrs. Stanard, the Helen of Poe's youth, but to Sarah Helen Whitman—"Helen—my Helen—the Helen of a thousand dreams," as Poe wrote in one of his importunate letters. "An Enigma" is a sonnet so constructed that the first letter of the first line, the second letter of the second line, etc., spell the name "Sarah Anna Lewis," another of Poe's fitful flames and a minor poet of whom he mendaciously wrote: "Mrs. Lewis is, perhaps, the best educated, if not the most accomplished of American authoresses." "A Valentine" employs the same device; but this time the concealed letters combine to spell the name "Frances Sargent Osgood," another of the lady literati who had stirred Poe's volcanic nature.

Of the variously dedicated poems the most important is "For Annie." Annie was Mrs. Annie Richmond of Lowell, Massachusetts, with whom Poe fell desperately in love while he was winning Sarah Helen Whitman of Providence. The macabre tone is appropriately that of the death-bed, for Poe was not only contemplating but attempting suicide at the time of its composition. The same Annie may well have been the inspiration of "Annabel Lee," although Mrs. Whitman thought it referred to herself, and some editors have insisted that it is sacrilege to connect the poem with anyone but Poe's lost Virginia.

"The Bells," poetry's most famous example of echolalia, originally consisted of eighteen lines; Poe expanded them to more than a hundred. It remains a question whether the enlargement produced "the most resounding poem in all literature" or "not a poem at all, but a game." It still has the unquestionable power of filling the ear and firing the imagination.

Annabel Lee

It was many and many a year ago,
    In a kingdom by the sea,
That a maiden there lived whom you may know
    By the name of ANNABEL LEE;
And this maiden she lived with no other thought
    Than to love and be loved by me.

I was a child and she was a child,
    In this kingdom by the sea;
But we loved with a love that was more than love—
    I and my Annabel Lee;
With a love that the wingèd seraphs of heaven
    Coveted her and me.

And this was the reason that, long ago,
    In this kingdom by the sea,
A wind blew out of a cloud, chilling
    My beautiful Annabel Lee;
So that her highborn kinsman came
    And bore her away from me,
To shut her up in a sepulchre
    In this kingdom by the sea.

The angels, not half so happy in heaven,
    Went envying her and me—
Yes!—that was the reason (as all men know,
    In this kingdom by the sea)
That the wind came out of the cloud by night,
    Chilling and killing my Annabel Lee.

But our love it was stronger by far than the love
    Of those who were older than we—
    Of many far wiser than we—
And neither the angels in heaven above,
    Nor the demons down under the sea,
Can ever dissever my soul from the soul
    Of the beautiful Annabel Lee.

For the moon never beams without bringing me dreams
    Of the beautiful Annabel Lee;
And the stars never rise but I feel the bright eyes
    Of the beautiful Annabel Lee;

And so, all the night-tide, I lie down by the side
Of my darling—my darling—my life and my bride,
In the sepulchre there by the sea,
In her tomb by the sounding sea.

To —— ——

Not long ago, the writer of these lines,
In the mad pride of intellectuality,
Maintained "the power of words"—denied that ever
A thought arose within the human brain
Beyond the utterance of the human tongue:
And now, as if in mockery of that boast,
Two words—two foreign soft dissyllables—
Italian tones, made only to be murmured
By angels dreaming in the moonlit "dew
That hangs like chains of pearl on Hermon hill,"
Have stirred from out the abysses of his heart,
Unthought-like thoughts that are the souls of thought,
Richer, far wilder, far diviner visions
Than even seraph harper, Israfel,
(Who has "the sweetest voice of all God's creatures,")
Could hope to utter. And I! my spells are broken.
The pen falls powerless from my shivering hand.
With thy dear name as text, though bidden by thee,
I cannot write—I cannot speak or think—
Alas, I cannot feel; for 'tis not feeling,
This standing motionless upon the golden
Threshold of the wide-open gate of dreams.
Gazing, entranced, adown the gorgeous vista,
And thrilling as I see, upon the right,
Upon the left, and all the way along,
Amid empurpled vapors, far away
To where the prospect terminates—*thee only*.

For Annie

Thank Heaven! the crisis—
    The danger is past,
And the lingering illness
    Is over at last—
And the fever called "Living"
    Is conquered at last.

Sadly, I know
    I am shorn of my strength,
And no muscle I move
    As I lie at full length—
But no matter!—I feel
    I am better at length.

And I rest so composedly,
    Now, in my bed,
That any beholder
    Might fancy me dead—
Might start at beholding me,
    Thinking me dead.

The moaning and groaning,
    The sighing and sobbing,
Are quieted now,
    With that horrible throbbing
At heart:—ah, that horrible,
    Horrible throbbing!

The sickness—the nausea—
    The pitiless pain—
Have ceased, with the fever
    That maddened my brain—
With the fever called "Living"
    That burned in my brain.

And oh! of all tortures
    That torture the worst
Has abated—the terrible
    Torture of thirst
For the naphthaline river
    Of Passion accurst:—
I have drunk of a water
    That quenches all thirst:—

Of a water that flows,
    With a lullaby sound,

[FOR ANNIE]

From a spring but a very few
 Feet under ground—
From a cavern not very far
 Down under ground.

And ah! let it never
 Be foolishly said
That my room it is gloomy
 And narrow my bed;
For man never slept
 In a different bed—
And, *to sleep,* you must slumber
 In just such a bed.

My tantalized spirit
 Here blandly reposes,
Forgetting, or never
 Regretting its roses—
Its old agitations
 Of myrtles and roses:

For now, while so quietly
 Lying, it fancies
A holier odor
 About it, of pansies—
A rosemary odor,
 Commingled with pansies—
With rue and the beautiful
 Puritan pansies.

And so it lies happily,
 Bathing in many
A dream of the truth
 And the beauty of Annie—
Drowned in a bath
 Of the tresses of Annie.

She tenderly kissed me,
 She fondly caressed,
And then I fell gently
 To sleep on her breast—
Deeply to sleep
 From the heaven of her breast.

188

When the light was extinguished,
   She covered me warm,
And she prayed to the angels
   To keep me from harm—
To the queen of the angels
   To shield me from harm.

And I lie so composedly,
   Now, in my bed,
(Knowing her love)
   That you fancy me dead—
And I rest so contentedly,
   Now, in my bed,
(With her love at my breast)
   That you fancy me dead—
That you shudder to look at me,
   Thinking me dead.

But my heart it is brighter
   Than all of the many
Stars in the sky,
   For it sparkles with Annie—
It glows with the light
   Of the love of my Annie—
With the thought of the light
   Of the eyes of my Annie.

An Enigma

"Seldom we find," says Solomon Don Dunce,
   "Half an idea in the profoundest sonnet.
Through all the flimsy things we see at once
   As easily as through a Naples bonnet—
   Trash of all trash!—how *can* a lady don it?
Yet heavier far than your Petrarchan stuff—
Owl-downy nonsense that the faintest puff
   Twirls into trunk-paper the while you con it."
And, veritably, Sol is right enough.
The general tuckermanities are arrant
Bubbles—ephemeral and *so* transparent—
   But *this* is, now—you may depend upon it—
Stable, opaque, immortal—all by dint
Of the dear names that lie concealed within 't.

The Bells

Hear the sledges with the bells—
         Silver bells!
What a world of merriment their melody foretells!
      How they tinkle, tinkle, tinkle,
         In the icy air of night!
      While the stars that oversprinkle
      All the heavens, seem to twinkle
         With a crystalline delight;
      Keeping time, time, time,
      In a sort of Runic rhyme,
To the tintinnabulation that so musically wells
      From the bells, bells, bells, bells,
         Bells, bells, bells—
From the jingling and the tinkling of the bells.

      Hear the mellow wedding bells,
         Golden bells!
What a world of happiness their harmony foretells!
      Through the balmy air of night
      How they ring out their delight!
         From the molten-golden notes,
         And all in tune,
      What a liquid ditty floats
To the turtle-dove that listens, while she gloats
         On the moon!
      Oh, from out the sounding cells,
What a gush of euphony voluminously wells!
         How it swells!
         How it dwells
      On the Future! how it tells
      Of the rapture that impels
      To the swinging and the ringing
         Of the bells, bells, bells,
      Of the bells, bells, bells, bells,
         Bells, bells, bells—
To the rhyming and the chiming of the bells!

      Hear the loud alarum bells—
         Brazen bells!
What a tale of terror, now, their turbulency tells!
      In the startled ear of night

How they scream out their affright!
Too much horrified to speak,
They can only shriek, shriek,
Out of tune,
In a clamorous appealing to the mercy of the fire,
In a mad expostulation with the deaf and frantic fire,
Leaping higher, higher, higher,
With a desperate desire,
And a resolute endeavor,
Now—now to sit or never,
By the side of the pale-faced moon.
Oh, the bells, bells, bells!
What a tale their terror tells
Of Despair!
How they clang, and clash, and roar!
What a horror they outpour
On the bosom of the palpitating air!
Yet the ear it fully knows,
By the twanging,
And the clanging,
How the danger ebbs and flows:
Yet the ear distinctly tells,
In the jangling,
And the wrangling,
How the danger sinks and swells,
By the sinking or the swelling in the anger of the bells—
Of the bells—
Of the bells, bells, bells, bells,
Bells, bells, bells—
In the clamor and the clangor of the bells!

IV

Hear the tolling of the bells—
Iron bells!
What a world of solemn thought their monody compels!
In the silence of the night,
How we shiver with affright
At the melancholy menace of their tone!
For every sound that floats
From the rust within their throats
Is a groan.
And the people—ah, the people—
They that dwell up in the steeple,
All alone,
And who, tolling, tolling, tolling,

In that muffled monotone,
Feel a glory in so rolling
    On the human heart a stone—
They are neither man nor woman—
They are neither brute nor human—
        They are Ghouls:
    And their king it is who tolls;
    And he rolls, rolls, rolls,
            Rolls
        A paean from the bells!
And his merry bosom swells
    With the paean of the bells!
And he dances, and he yells;
Keeping time, time, time,
In a sort of Runic rhyme,
    To the paean of the bells—
        Of the bells:
Keeping time, time, time,
In a sort of Runic rhyme,
    To the throbbing of the bells—
Of the bells, bells, bells—
    To the sobbing of the bells;
Keeping time, time, time,
    As he knells, knells, knells,
In a happy Runic rhyme,
    To the rolling of the bells—
Of the bells, bells, bells:
    To the tolling of the bells,
Of the bells, bells, bells, bells—
    Bells, bells, bells—
To the moaning and the groaning of the bells.

To M. L. S——

Of all who hail thy presence as the morning—
Of all to whom thine absence is the night—
The blotting utterly from out high heaven
The sacred sun—of all who, weeping, bless thee
Hourly for hope—for life—ah! above all,
For the resurrection of deep-buried faith
In Truth—in Virtue—in Humanity—
Of all who, on Despair's unhallowed bed
Lying down to die, have suddenly arisen
At thy soft-murmured words, "Let there be light!"
At the soft-murmured words that were fulfilled
In the seraphic glancing of thine eyes—
Of all who owe thee most—whose gratitude
Nearest resembles worship—oh, remember
The truest—the most fervently devoted,
And think that these weak lines are written by him—
By him who, as he pens them, thrills to think
His spirit is communing with an angel's.

Ulalume

The skies they were ashen and sober;
    The leaves they were crisped and sere—
    The leaves they were withering and sere;
It was night in the lonesome October
    Of my most immemorial year;
It was hard by the dim lake of Auber,
    In the misty mid region of Weir—
It was down by the dank tarn of Auber,
    In the ghoul-haunted woodland of Weir.

Here once, through an alley Titanic,
    Of cypress, I roamed with my Soul—
    Of cypress, with Psyche, my Soul.
There were days when my heart was volcanic
    As the scoriac rivers that roll—
    As the lavas that restlessly roll
Their sulphurous currents down Yaanek
    In the ultimate climes of the pole—
That groan as they roll down Mount Yaanek
    In the realms of the boreal pole.

Our talk had been serious and sober,
    But our thoughts they were palsied and sere—
    Our memories were treacherous and sere—
For we knew not the month was October,
    And we marked not the night of the year—
    (Ah, night of all nights in the year!)
We noted not the dim lake of Auber—
    (Though once we had journeyed down here),
Remembered not the dank tarn of Auber,
    Nor the ghoul-haunted woodland of Weir.

And now, as the night was senescent,
    And star-dials pointed to morn—
    As the star-dials hinted of morn—
At the end of our path a liquescent
    And nebulous lustre was born,
Out of which a miraculous crescent
    Arose with a duplicate horn—
Astarte's bediamonded crescent
    Distinct with its duplicate horn.

And I said—"She is warmer than Dian:
    She rolls through an ether of sighs—

ULALUME

She revels in a region of sighs:
She has seen that the tears are not dry on
These cheeks, where the worm never dies,
And has come past the stars of the Lion,
To point us the path to the skies—
To the Lethean peace of the skies—
Come up, in despite of the Lion,
To shine on us with her bright eyes—
Come up through the lair of the Lion,
With love in her luminous eyes."

But Psyche, uplifting her finger,
Said—"Sadly this star I mistrust—
Her pallor I strangely mistrust:—
Oh, hasten!—oh, let us not linger!
Oh, fly!—let us fly!—for we must."
In terror she spoke, letting sink her
Wings until they trailed in the dust—
In agony sobbed, letting sink her
Plumes till they trailed in the dust—
Till they sorrowfully trailed in the dust.

I replied—"This is nothing but dreaming:
Let us on by this tremulous light!
Let us bathe in this crystalline light!
Its Sybilic splendor is beaming
With Hope and in Beauty to-night:—
See!—it flickers up the sky through the night!
Ah, we safely may trust to its gleaming,
And be sure it will lead us aright—
We safely may trust to a gleaming
That cannot but guide us aright,
Since it flickers up to Heaven through the night."

Thus I pacified Psyche and kissed her,
And tempted her out of her gloom—
And conquered her scruples and gloom;
And we passed to the end of the vista,
But were stopped by the door of a tomb—
By the door of a legended tomb;
And I said—"What is written, sweet sister,
On the door of this legended tomb?"
She replied—"Ulalume—Ulalume—
'Tis the vault of thy lost Ulalume!"

Then my heart it grew ashen and sober
As the leaves that were crisped and sere—
As the leaves that were withering and sere—
And I cried—"It was surely October
On *this* very night of last year
That I journeyed—I journeyed down here—
That I brought a dread burden down here—
On this night of all nights in the year,
Ah, what demon has tempted me here?
Well I know, now, this dim lake of Auber—
This misty mid region of Weir—
Well I know, now, this dank tarn of Auber,
This ghoul-haunted woodland of Weir."

Eldorado

Gaily bedight,
A gallant knight,
In sunshine and in shadow,
Had journeyed long,
Singing a song,
In search of Eldorado.

But he grew old—
This knight so bold—
And o'er his heart a shadow
Fell as he found
No spot of ground
That looked like Eldorado.

And, as his strength
Failed him at length,
He met a pilgrim shadow—
"Shadow," said he,
"Where can it be—
This land of Eldorado?"

"Over the Mountains
Of the Moon,
Down the Valley of the Shadow,
Ride, boldly ride,"
The shade replied—
"If you seek for Eldorado!"

To Helen

I saw thee once—once only—years ago:
I must not say *how* many—but *not* many.
It was a July midnight; and from out
A full-orbed moon, that, like thine own soul, soaring,
Sought a precipitate pathway up through heaven,
There fell a silvery-silken veil of light,
With quietude, and sultriness, and slumber,
Upon the upturned faces of a thousand
Roses that grew in an enchanted garden,
Where no wind dared to stir, unless on tiptoe—
Fell on the upturn'd faces of these roses
That gave out, in return for the love-light,
Their odorous souls in an ecstatic death—
Fell on the upturn'd faces of these roses
That smiled and died in this parterre, enchanted
By thee, and by the poetry of thy presence.

Clad all in white, upon a violet bank
I saw thee half reclining; while the moon
Fell on the upturn'd faces of the roses,
And on thine own, upturn'd—alas, in sorrow!

Was it not Fate, that, on this July midnight—
Was it not Fate, (whose name is also Sorrow,)
That bade me pause before that garden-gate,
To breathe the incense of those slumbering roses?
No footstep stirred: the hated world all slept,
Save only thee and me. (Oh, Heaven!—oh, God!
How my heart beats in coupling those two words!)
Save only thee and me. I paused—I looked—
And in an instant all things disappeared.
(Ah, bear in mind this garden was enchanted!)

The pearly lustre of the moon went out:
The mossy banks and the meandering paths,
The happy flowers and the repining trees,
Were seen no more: the very roses' odors
Died in the arms of the adoring airs.
All—all expired save thee—save less than thou:
Save only the divine light in thine eyes—
Save but the soul in thine uplifted eyes.
I saw but them—they were the world to me!
I saw but them—saw only them for hours,
Saw only them until the moon went down.

What wild heart-histories seemed to lie enwritten
Upon those crystalline, celestial spheres!
How dark a woe, yet how sublime a hope!
How silently serene a sea of pride!
How daring an ambition; yet how deep—
How fathomless a capacity for love!

But now, at length, dear Dian sank from sight,
Into a western couch of thunder-cloud;
And thou, a ghost, amid the entombing trees
Didst glide away. *Only thine eyes remained;*
They *would not go*—they never yet have gone;
Lighting my lonely pathway home that night,
They have not left me (as my hopes have) since;
They follow me—they lead me through the years.
They are my ministers—yet I their slave.
Their office is to illumine and enkindle—
My duty, *to be saved* by their bright light,
And purified in their electric fire,
And sanctified in their elysian fire.
They fill my soul with Beauty (which is Hope),
And are far up in Heaven—the stars I kneel to
In the sad, silent watches of my night;
While even in the meridian glare of day
I see them still—two sweetly scintillant
Venuses, unextinguished by the sun!

To My Mother

Because I feel that, in the Heavens above,
　　The angels, whispering to one another,
Can find, among their burning terms of love,
　　None so devotional as that of "Mother,"
Therefore by that dear name I long have called you—
　　You who are more than mother unto me,
And fill my heart of hearts, where Death installed you
　　In setting my Virginia's spirit free.
My mother—my own mother, who died early,
　　Was but the mother of myself; but you
Are mother to the one I loved so dearly,
　　And thus are dearer than the mother I knew
By that infinity with which my wife
　　Was dearer to my soul than its soul-life.

A Valentine

For her this rhyme is penned, whose luminous eyes,
    Brightly expressive as the twins of Leda,
Shall find her own sweet name, that nestling lies
    Upon the page, enwrapped from every reader.
Search narrowly the lines!—they hold a treasure
    Divine—a talisman—an amulet
That must be worn *at heart*. Search well the measure—
    The words—the syllables! Do not forget
The trivialest point, or you may lose your labor!
    And yet there is in this no Gordian knot
Which one might not undo without a sabre,
    If one could merely comprehend the plot.
Enwritten upon the leaf where now are peering
    Eyes scintillating soul, there lie *perdus*
Three eloquent words oft uttered in the hearing
    Of poets, by poets—as the name is a poet's, too,
Its letters, although naturally lying
    Like the knight Pinto—Mendez Ferdinando—
Still form a synonym for Truth—Cease trying!
    You will not read the riddle, though you do the best you *can* do.

Alone

From childhood's hour I have not been
As others were; I have not seen
As others saw; I could not bring
My passions from a common spring.
From the same source I have not taken
My sorrow; I could not awaken
My heart to joy at the same tone;
And all I loved, *I* loved alone.
Then—in my childhood, in the dawn
Of a most stormy life—was drawn
From every depth of good and ill
The mystery which binds me still:
From the torrent, or the fountain,
From the red cliff of the mountain,
From the sun that round me rolled
In its autumn tint of gold,
From the lightning in the sky
As it passed me flying by,
From the thunder and the storm,
And the cloud that took the form
(When the rest of Heaven was blue)
Of a demon in my view.

The Poems of Edgar Allan Poe

IX

THE PHILOSOPHY OF COMPOSITION

[AN ESSAY]

The Editor's Commentary

MOST OF THE commentators refuse to accept "The Philosophy of Composition" at its face value. Some of Poe's critics dismiss it as an artificial deception, a deliberate hoax. Others regard it as an ingenious exercise in the art of rationalization, a clever but unsuccessful attempt to convince the reader that Poe's works, and especially "The Raven," were produced by precise logic, with (as Poe claimed) "the rigid consequence of a mathematical problem." Speaking for the majority, Joseph Wood Krutch, in *Edgar Allan Poe: A Study in Genius*, maintained, "No writer who ever lived seems less likely than Poe to have created in this way. In the management of his own life, he was moved almost always by prejudice, passion, or perversity, and almost never by reason. His works, characterized at their best by the fantastic illogicality of dreams, are such as no man could *contrive*."

Yet contrivance was not only part of Poe's genius, it was part of his craft. Nothing could be more logical than Poe's methodical explanation of the automatic chess-player, his skillful solutions of involved cryptograms, and, most significantly, his invention of—and identification with—the coldly rational detective, model for all the succeeding masters of deduction from Sherlock Holmes to Nero Wolfe.

The conflicting accounts of the composition of "The Raven" have never been reconciled. But it is possible to believe that, in "The Philosophy of Composition," Poe was more justifiably logical than his critics. The ideas and effects may not have come to home all at once, but they were there, present in his subconsciousness, waiting to be integrated by the conscious craftsman. It needed only the moment of integration to unite the various "devices": the bird of Pallas Athena, changed from the original owl to Barnaby Rudge's raven as an emblem of never-ending remembrance; the elegiac refrain with its mournfully sonorous "Nevermore"; the deliberate choice of a theme which was, to Poe, the most universal and poetical of all themes: the death of a beautiful woman.

It will always be argued that "The Philosophy of Composition" is a rationalization after the event, that, here as elsewhere, Poe made his own limitations the law of art. Yet here, as elsewhere, Poe resolved his contradictions. As a critic, he was bedevilled by the conflict between Truth and Beauty. As a poet, he reconciled the rival claims.

The Philosophy of Composition

CHARLES DICKENS, in a note now lying before me, alluding to an examination I once made of the mechanism of "Barnaby Rudge," says: "By the way, are you aware that Godwin wrote his 'Caleb Williams' backward? He first involved his hero in a web of difficulties, forming the second volume, and then, for the first, cast about him for some mode of accounting for what had been done."

I cannot think this the *precise* mode of procedure on the part of Godwin—and indeed what he himself acknowledges is not altogether in accordance with Mr. Dickens' idea; but the author of "Caleb Williams" was too good an artist not to perceive the advantage derivable from at least a somewhat similar process. Nothing is more clear than that every plot, worth the name, must be elaborated to its *dénouement* before anything be attempted with the pen. It is only with the *dénouement* constantly in view that we can give a plot its indispensable air of consequence, or causation, by making the incidents, and especially the tone at all points, tend to the development of the intention.

There is a radical error, I think, in the usual mode of constructing a story. Either history affords a thesis—or one is suggested by an incident of the day—or, at best, the author sets himself to work in the combination of striking events to form merely the basis of his narrative—designing, generally, to fill in with description, dialogue, or authorial comment, whatever crevices of fact, or action, may, from page to page, render themselves apparent.

I prefer commencing with the consideration of an *effect*. Keeping originality *always* in view—for he is false to himself who ventures to dispense with so obvious and so easily attainable a source of interest—I say to myself, in the first place: "Of the innumerable effects, or impressions, of which the heart, the intellect, or (more generally) the soul is susceptible, what one shall I, on the present occasion, select?" Having chosen a novel, first, and secondly a vivid effect, I consider whether it can be best wrought by incident or tone—whether by ordinary incidents and peculiar tone, or the converse, or by peculiarity both of incident and tone—afterward looking about me (or rather within) for such combinations of event, or tone, as shall best aid me in the construction of the effect.

I have often thought how interesting a magazine paper might be written by any author who would—that is to say, who could—detail, step by step, the processes by which any one of his compositions attained its ultimate point of completion. Why such a paper has never been given to the world, I am much at a loss to say—but, perhaps, the authorial vanity has had more to do with the omission than any one other cause. Most writers—poets in especial—prefer having it understood that they compose by a species of fine frenzy—an ecstatic intuition—and would positively shudder at letting the public take a peep behind the scenes, at the elaborate and vacillating crudities of thought —at the true purposes seized only at the last moment—at the innumerable glimpses of idea that arrived not at the maturity of full view— at the fully matured fancies discarded in despair as unmanageable— at the cautious selections and rejections—at the painful erasures and interpolations—in a word, at the wheels and pinions—the tackle for scene-shifting—the step-ladders and demon-traps, the cock's feathers, the red paint and the black patches, which, in ninety-nine cases out of the hundred, constitute the properties of the literary *histrio*.

I am aware, on the other hand, that the case is by no means common, in which an author is at all in condition to retrace the steps by which his conclusions have been attained. In general, suggestions, having arisen pell-mell, are pursued and forgotten in a similar manner.

For my own part, I have neither sympathy with the repugnance alluded to, nor, at any time, the least difficulty in recalling to mind the progressive steps of any of my compositions; and, since the interest of an analysis, or reconstruction, such as I have considered a *desideratum*, is quite independent of any real or fancied interest in the thing analysed, it will not be regarded as a breach of decorum on my part to show the *modus operandi* by which some one of my own works was put together. I select "The Raven" as most generally known. It is my design to render it manifest that no one point in its composition is referable either to accident or intuition—that the work proceeded, step by step, to its completion with the precision and rigid consequence of a mathematical problem.

Let us dismiss, as irrelevant to the poem *per se*, the circumstance —or say the necessity—which, in the first place, gave rise to the intention of composing *a* poem that should suit at once the popular and the critical taste.

We commence, then, with this intention.

The initial consideration was that of extent. If any literary work is too long to be read at one sitting, we must be content to dispense with the immensely important effect derivable from unity of impression— for, if two sittings be required, the affairs of the world interfere, and everything like totality is at once destroyed. But since, *ceteris paribus*, no poet can afford to dispense with *anything* that may advance his design, it but remains to be seen whether there is, in extent, any advantage to counterbalance the loss of unity which attends it. Here I say no, at once. What we term a long poem is, in fact, merely a succession of brief ones—that is to say, of brief poetical effects. It is needless to demonstrate that a poem is such, only inasmuch as it intensely excites, by elevating, the soul; and all intense excitements are, through a physical necessity, brief. For this reason, at least one-half of the "Paradise Lost" is essentially prose—a succession of poetical excitements interspersed, *inevitably*, with corresponding depressions—the whole being deprived, through the extremeness of its length, of the vastly important artistic element, totality, or unity, of effect.

It appears evident, then, that there is a distinct limit, as regards length, to all works of literary art—the limit of a single sitting—and that, although in certain classes of prose composition, such as "Robinson Crusoe" (demanding no unity), this limit may be advantageously overpassed, it can never properly be overpassed in a poem. Within this limit, the extent of a poem may be made to bear mathematical relation to its merit—in other words, to the excitement or elevation—again, in other words, to the degree of the true poetical effect which it is capable of inducing; for it is clear that the brevity must be in direct ratio of the intensity of the intended effect:—this, with one proviso—that a certain degree of duration is absolutely requisite for the production of any effect at all.

Holding in view these considerations, as well as that degree of excitement which I deemed not above the popular, while not below the critical, taste, I reached at once what I conceived the proper *length* for my intended poem, a length of about one hundred lines. It is, in fact, a hundred and eight.

My next thought concerned the choice of an impression, or effect, to be conveyed; and here I may as well observe that, throughout the construction, I kept steadily in view the design of rendering the work *universally* appreciable. I should be carried too far out of my immediate topic were I to demonstrate a point upon which I have repeatedly insisted, and which, with the poetical, stands not in the slightest need of demonstration—the point, I mean, that Beauty is the sole legitimate province of the poem. A few words, however, in elucidation of my real meaning, which some of my friends have evinced a disposition to misrepresent. That pleasure which is at once the most intense, the most elevating, and the most pure, is, I believe, found in the contemplation of the beautiful. When, indeed, men speak of Beauty, they mean, precisely, not a quality, as is supposed, but an effect—they refer, in short, just to that intense and pure elevation of *soul*—*not* of intellect, or of heart—upon which I have commented, and which is experienced in consequence of contemplating "the beautiful." Now I designate Beauty as the province of the poem, merely because it is an obvious rule of Art that effects should be made to spring from direct causes—that objects should be attained through means best adapted for their attainment—no one as yet having been weak enough to deny that the peculiar elevation alluded to, is *most readily* attained in the poem. Now the object, Truth, or the satisfaction of the intellect, and the object Passion, or the excitement of the heart, are, although attainable, to a certain extent, in poetry, far more readily attainable in prose. Truth, in fact, demands a precision, and Passion a *homeliness* (the truly passionate will comprehend me), which are absolutely antagonistic to that Beauty which, I maintain, is the excitement, or pleasurable elevation, of the soul. It by no means follows from anything here said, that passion, or even truth, may not be introduced, and even profitably introduced, into a poem—for they may serve in elucidation, or aid the general effect, as do discords in music, by contrast—but the true artist will always contrive, first, to tone them into proper subservience to the predominant aim, and, secondly, to enveil them, as far as possible, in that Beauty which is the atmosphere and the essence of the poem.

Regarding, then, Beauty as my province, my next question referred to the *tone* of its highest manifestation—and all experience has shown that this tone is one of *sadness*. Beauty of whatever kind, in its supreme development, invariably excites the sensitive soul to tears. Melancholy is thus the most legitimate of all the poetical tones.

The length, the province, and the tone, being thus determined, I betook myself to ordinary induction, with the view of obtaining some artistic piquancy which might serve me as a key-note in the construction of the poem—some pivot upon which the whole structure might turn. In carefully thinking over all the usual artistic effects—or more properly *points*, in the theatrical sense—I did not fail to perceive immediately that no one had been so universally employed as that of the *refrain*. The universality of its employment sufficed to assure me of its intrinsic value, and spared me the necessity of submitting it to analysis. I considered it, however, with regard to its susceptibility of improvement, and soon saw it to be in a primitive condition. As commonly used, the *refrain*, or burden, not only is limited to lyric verse, but depends for its impression upon the force of monotone—both in sound and thought. The pleasure is deduced solely from the sense of identity—of repetition. I resolved to diversify, and so heighten, the effect, by adhering, in general, to the monotone of sound, while I continually varied that of thought: that is to say, I determined to produce continuously novel effects, by the variation *of the application* of the *refrain*—the *refrain* itself remaining, for the most part, unvaried.

These points being settled, I next bethought me of the *nature* of my *refrain*. Since its application was to be repeatedly varied, it was clear that the *refrain* itself must be brief, for there would have been an insurmountable difficulty in frequent variations of application in any sentence of length. In proportion to the brevity of the sentence, would, of course, be the facility of the variation. This led me at once to a single word as the best *refrain*.

The question now arose as to the *character* of the word. Having made up my mind to a *refrain*, the division of the poem into stanzas was, of course, a corollary: the *refrain* forming the close to each stanza. That such a close, to have force, must be sonorous and susceptible of protracted emphasis, admitted no doubt; and these considerations inevitably led me to the long *o* as the most sonorous vowel, in connection with *r* as the most producible consonant.

The sound of the *refrain* being thus determined, it became necessary to select a word embodying this sound, and at the same time in the fullest possible keeping with that melancholy which I had predetermined as the tone of the poem. In such a search it would have been absolutely impossible to overlook the word "Nevermore." In fact, it was the very first which presented itself.

The next *desideratum* was a pretext for the continuous use of the one word "Nevermore." In observing the difficulty which I at once found in inventing a sufficiently plausible reason for its continuous repetition, I did not fail to perceive that this difficulty arose solely from the pre-assumption that the word was to be so continuously or monotonously spoken by a *human* being—I did not fail to perceive, in short, that the difficulty lay in the reconciliation of this monotony with the exercise of reason on the part of the creature repeating the word. Here, then, immediately arose the idea of a *non*-reasoning creature capable of speech; and, very naturally, a parrot, in the first instance, suggested itself, but was superseded forthwith by a Raven, as equally capable of speech, and infinitely more in keeping with the intended *tone*.

I had now gone so far as the conception of a Raven—the bird of ill omen—monotonously repeating the one word, "Nevermore," at the conclusion of each stanza, in a poem of melancholy tone, and in length about one hundred lines. Now, never losing sight of the object *supremeness*, or perfection, at all points, I asked myself: "Of all melancholy topics, what, according to the *universal* understanding of mankind, is the *most* melancholy?" Death—was the obvious reply. "And when," I said, "is this most melancholy of topics most poetical?" From what I have already explained at some length, the answer, here also, is obvious—"When it most closely allies itself to *Beauty:* the death, then, of a beautiful woman is, unquestionably, the most poetical topic in the world—and equally is it beyond doubt that the lips best suited for such topic are those of a bereaved lover."

I had now to combine the two ideas, of a lover lamenting his deceased mistress and a Raven continuously repeating the word "Nevermore." I had to combine these, bearing in mind my design of varying, at every turn, the *application* of the word repeated; but the only intelligible mode of such combination is that of imagining the Raven employing the word in answer to the queries of the lover. And here it was that I saw at once the opportunity afforded for the effect on which I had been depending—that is to say, the effect of the *variation of application*. I saw that I could make the first query propounded by the lover—the first query to which the Raven should reply "Nevermore" —that I could make this first query a commonplace one—the second less so—the third still less, and so on—until at length the lover, startled from his original *nonchalance* by the melancholy character of the word itself—by its frequent repetition—and by a consideration of the ominous reputation of the fowl that uttered it—is at length excited to superstition, and wildly propounds queries of a far different character —queries whose solution he has passionately at heart—propounds them half in superstition and half in that species of despair which delights in self-torture—propounds them not altogether because he believes in the prophetic or demoniac character of the bird (which, reason assures him, is merely repeating a lesson learned by rote), but because he experiences a frenzied pleasure in so modelling his questions as to receive from the *expected* "Nevermore" the most delicious, because the most intolerable, of sorrow. Perceiving the opportunity thus afforded me—or, more strictly, thus forced upon me in the progress of the construction—I first established in mind the climax, or concluding query—that query to which "Nevermore" should be in the last place an answer—that query in reply to which this word "Nevermore" should involve the utmost conceivable amount of sorrow and despair.

Here, then, the poem may be said to have its beginning—at the end, where all works of art should begin—for it was here, at this point of my preconsiderations, that I first put pen to paper in the composition of the stanza:

> "Prophet," said I, "thing of evil! prophet still if bird or devil!
> By that heaven that bends above us—by that God we both adore,
> Tell this soul with sorrow laden, if within the distant Aidenn,
> It shall clasp a sainted maiden whom the angels name Lenore—
> Clasp a rare and radiant maiden whom the angels name Lenore."
>   Quoth the raven "Nevermore."

I composed this stanza, at this point, first that, by establishing the climax, I might the better vary and graduate, as regards seriousness and importance, the preceding queries of the lover—and, secondly, that I might definitely settle the rhythm, the metre, and the length and general arrangement of the stanza—as well as graduate the stanzas which were to precede, so that none of them might surpass this in rhythmical effect. Had I been able, in the subsequent composition, to construct more vigorous stanzas, I should, without scruple, have

210

purposely enfeebled them, so as not to interfere with the climacteric effect.

And here I may as well say a few words of the versification. My first object (as usual) was originality. The extent to which this has been neglected, in versification, is one of the most unaccountable things in the world. Admitting that there is little possibility of variety in mere *rhythm*, it is still clear that the possible varieties of metre and stanza are absolutely infinite—and yet, *for centuries, no man, in verse, has ever done, or ever seemed to think of doing, an original thing.* The fact is, that originality (unless in minds of very unusual force) is by no means a matter, as some suppose, of impulse or intuition. In general, to be found, it must be elaborately sought, and although a positive merit of the highest class, demands in its attainment less of invention than negation.

Of course, I pretend to no originality in either the rhythm or metre of "the Raven." The former is trochaic—the latter is octameter acatalectic, alternating with heptameter catalectic repeated in the *refrain* of the fifth verse, and terminating with tetrameter catalectic. Less pedantically—the feet employed through (trochees) consist of a long syllable followed by a short: the first line of the stanza consists of eight of these feet—the second of seven and a half (in effect two-thirds) —the third of eight—the fourth of seven and a half—the fifth the same—the sixth three and a half. Now, each of these lines, taken individually, has been employed before, and what originality the "Raven" has, is in the *combination into stanza;* nothing even remotely approaching this combination has ever been attempted. The effect of this originality of combination is aided by other unusual, and some altogether novel effects, arising from an extension of the application of the principles of rhyme and alliteration.

The next point to be considered was the mode of bringing together the lover and the Raven—and the first branch of this consideration was the *locale.* For this the most natural suggestion might seem to be a forest, or the fields—but it has always appeared to me that a close *circumscription of space* is absolutely necessary to the effect of insulated incident:—it has the force of a frame to a picture. It has an indisputable moral power in keeping concentrated the attention, and, of course, must not be confounded with mere unity of place.

I determined, then, to place the lover in his chamber—in a chamber rendered sacred to him by memories of her who had frequented it. The room is represented as richly furnished—this is mere pursuance of the ideas I have already explained on the subject of Beauty, as the sole true poetical thesis.

The *locale* being thus determined, I had now to introduce the bird —and the thought of introducing him through the window, was inevitable. The idea of making the lover suppose, in the first instance, that the flapping of the wings of the bird against the shutter, is a "tapping" at the door, originated in a wish to increase, by prolonging, the reader's curiosity, and in a desire to admit the incidental effect arising from the lover's throwing open the door, finding all dark, and thence adopting the half-fancy that it was the spirit of his mistress that knocked.

I made the night tempestuous, first, to account for the Raven's seeking admission, and secondly, for the effect of contrast with the (physical) serenity within the chamber.

I made the bird alight on the bust of Pallas, also for the effect of contrast between the marble and the plumage—it being understood that the bust was absolutely *suggested* by the bird—the bust of *Pallas* being chosen, first, as most in keeping with the scholarship of the lover, and, secondly, for the sonorousness of the word, Pallas, itself.

About the middle of the poem, also, I have availed myself of the force of contrast, with a view of deepening the ultimate impression. For example, an air of the fantastic—approaching as nearly to the ludicrous as was admissible—is given to the Raven's entrance. He comes in "with many a flirt and flutter."

Not the *least obeisance made he*—not a moment stopped or stayed he,
But with mien of lord or lady, perched above my chamber door.

In the two stanzas which follow, the design is more obviously carried out:—

Then this ebony bird beguiling my sad fancy into smiling
By the *grave and stern decorum of the countenance it wore*,
"Though thy *crest be shorn and shaven*, thou," I said, "art sure no
      craven,
Ghastly grim and ancient Raven wandering from the nightly shore—
Tell me what thy lordly name is on the Night's Plutonian shore?"
          Quoth the Raven "Nevermore."

Much I marvelled *this ungainly fowl* to hear discourse so plainly,
Though its answer little meaning—little relevancy bore;
For we cannot help agreeing that no living human being
Ever yet was blest with seeing bird above his chamber door—
Bird or beast upon the sculptured bust above his chamber door,
          With such name as "Nevermore."

The effect of the *dénouement* being thus provided for, I immediately drop the fantastic for a tone of the most profound seriousness:—

this tone commencing in the stanza directly following the one last quoted, with the line,

But the Raven, sitting lonely on that placid bust, spoke only, etc.

From this epoch the lover no longer jests—no longer sees anything even of the fantastic in the Raven's demeanor. He speaks of him as a "grim, ungainly, ghastly, gaunt, and ominous bird of yore," and feels the "fiery eyes" burning into his "bosom's core." This revolution of thought, or fancy, on the lover's part, is intended to induce a similar one on the part of the reader—to bring the mind into a proper frame for the *dénouement* which is now brought about as rapidly and as *directly* as possible.

With the *dénouement* proper—with the Raven's reply, "Nevermore," to the lover's final demand if he shall meet his mistress in another world—the poem, in its obvious phase, that of a simple narrative, may be said to have its completion. So far, everything is within the limits of the accountable—of the real. A raven, having learned by rote the single word "Nevermore," and having escaped from the custody of its owner, is driven at midnight, through the violence of a storm, to seek admission at a window from which a light still gleams—the chamber-window of a student, occupied half in poring over a volume, half in dreaming of a beloved mistress deceased. The casement being thrown open at the fluttering of a bird's wings, the bird itself perches on the most convenient seat out of the immediate reach of the student, who, amused by the incident and the oddity of the visitor's demeanor, demands of it, in jest and without looking for a reply, its name. The raven, addressed, answers with its customary word, "Nevermore"—a word which finds immediate echo in the melancholy heart of the student, who, giving utterance aloud to certain thoughts suggested by the occasion, is again startled by the fowl's repetition of "Nevermore." The student now guesses the state of the case, but is impelled, as I have before explained, by the human thirst for self-torture, and in part by superstition, to propound such queries to the bird as will bring him, the lover, the most of the luxury of sorrow, through the anticipated answer "Nevermore." With the indulgence, to the extreme, of this self-torture, the narration, in what I have termed its first or obvious phase, has a natural termination, and so far there has been no overstepping of the limits of the real.

But in subjects so handled, however skilfully, or with however vivid an array of incident, there is always a certain hardness or nakedness, which repels the artistical eye. Two things are invariably required—first, some amount of complexity, or more properly, adaptation; and, secondly, some amount of suggestiveness—some undercurrent, however indefinite, of meaning. It is this latter, in especial, which imparts to a work of art so much of that *richness* (to borrow from colloquy a forcible term) which we are too fond of confounding with *the ideal*. It is the *excess* of the suggested meaning—it is the rendering this the upper instead of the under-current of the theme—which turns into prose (and that of the very flattest kind) the so-called poetry of the so-called transcendentalists.

Holding these opinions, I added the two concluding stanzas of the poem—their suggestiveness being thus made to pervade all the narrative which has preceded them. The under-current of meaning is rendered first apparent in the lines—

"Take thy beak from out *my heart*, and take thy form from off my
  door!"
          Quoth the Raven "Nevermore!"

It will be observed that the words, "from out my heart," involve the first metaphorical expression in the poem. They, with the answer, "Nevermore," dispose the mind to seek a moral in all that has been previously narrated. The reader begins now to regard the Raven as emblematical—but it is not until the very last line of the very last stanza, that the intention of making him emblematical of *Mournful and Never-ending Remembrance* is permitted distinctly to be seen:

And the Raven, never flitting, still is sitting, still is sitting,
On the pallid bust of Pallas just above my chamber door;
And his eyes have all the seeming of a demon's that is dreaming,
And the lamplight o'er him streaming throws his shadow on the floor;
And my soul *from out that shadow* that lies floating on the floor
          Shall be lifted—nevermore.

To - Mary Coombs

Congratulations upon your
graduation —
all good wishes
    Jessie & Ted Rosebaugh
        June 1963